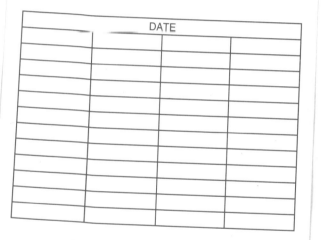

DATE			

THE NOAM CHOMSKY LECTURES

Daniel Brooks and Guillermo Verdecchia

Coach House Press
Toronto

Published with the assistance of the Canada Council,
the Ontario Arts Council, and the Ontario Ministry
of Culture and Communications.

The authors would like to acknowledge the following for their
invaluable assistance: Sky Gilbert and Buddies in Bad Times
Theatre, for giving us the opportunity to first perform the
play; the Augusta Company, David Demchuk, the Ontario
Arts Council, the Canada Council, Steven Bush, David
Groff, and Doug and Janette Pirie; Jason Sherman for his
undying support; and all the individuals who spoke to us
after performances to correct facts and challenge our
argument. We are indebted to Professors Noam Chomsky
and Edward S. Herman for much of the language and
analysis in the play. We assume sole responsibility
for any errors and inaccuracies.

The chart on page 18 is reprinted from Wallace Clement's
The Canadian Corporate Elite by permission of
Carleton University Press.

Canadian Cataloguing in Publication Data
Brooks, Daniel, 1958-
The Noam Chomsky lectures

A play.
ISBN 0-88910-413-1

1. Chomsky, Noam, in fiction, drama, poetry, etc.
I. Verdecchia, Guillermo. II. Title.

PS8553.R66N6 1991   C812'.54   C91-095043-1
PR9199.3.B76N6 1991

THIRD PRINTING

Contents

Introduction

Given the content of *The Noam Chomsky Lectures*, I want to say at the outset of this introduction that I have never met Brooks or Verdecchia (or Conlogue and Chapman, for that matter), do not (to my knowledge) appear in their sexual flow chart, nor do we bank at the same bank—theirs here revealed as the CIBC. And yet, I am a Biased Source. Not only have I often admired and sometimes utilized the work of Professor Chomsky, I am favourably disposed towards any work which tries to counter Blind Stupidity.

The Noam Chomsky Lectures takes on much more than the aforesaid B.S. And—in addition to being intelligent, funny, passionate, and filled with zippy pacing—this work is courageous.

Ordinarily, theatre relies on illusion in order to reveal truths. Brooks and Verdecchia's play—a "meta-theatrical explication," but a play nonetheless—relies on truths in order to reveal illusion. Such a reversal certainly risks the ire of the Esthetic Police, but *The Noam Chomsky Lectures* takes an even greater risk.

Like Chomsky himself, this work risks the assumption that the audience, "the public," is also intelligent, courageous, and willing to be more than the diminished ineffectual roles assigned to us by (in Eduardo Galeano's words) "a system organized to wipe us off the face of this earth, to disintegrate our souls, and to empty us of memory." In taking us through the Memory Hole, Brooks and Verdecchia help us retrieve not only lost strands of our own contemporary history, but also the concept of a public conscience.

The word "conscience" is a seemingly old-fashioned term

rarely heard any more, as though it belonged in the dustbin of historical diction along with quaint words such as "distaff" and "coxcombry." When the word is used at all, conscience is understood in our society to be a thoroughly private matter. And yet, the word's Latin root, *com + scire*, means "to know together"—an indication that the ability to make moral distinctions between right and wrong has something to do with community. Interestingly, the more often used word these days, "consciousness," has the same Latin root: a shared etymology that suggests a dialectic or dynamic interaction among awareness, conscience, and society.

As I recall, neither of these words, conscience or consciousness, is used in this work. *The Noam Chomsky Lectures* is more hip than that. And yet, it seems to me that this notion of "knowing together" is at the heart of the work, informing it and giving it energy. Following the impetus of Chomsky himself, Brooks and Verdecchia have recognized that mass media, mass spectacle, have trivialized and severed consciousness and conscience, separating both from a communal base. We collectively know little about what is done in our name by our elected governments and the business interests they serve.

The Noam Chomsky Lectures assumes not only that we *do* want to know, that our "knowing together" may change things, but also that it is less painful to know than to not know.

In one of her many books, Hannah Arendt has suggested that "the avoidance of ethical pain" is one of the great human drives: as strong, perhaps, as hunger. That avoidance, of course, may take either a negative or positive form. Negatively, such avoidance may be accomplished through denial and repression: a refusal to be conscious of the repercussions for others resulting from one's own decisions and actions. Positively, the avoidance of ethical pain takes place through the activation of conscience in advance of action. One is spared a greater degree of ethical pain by making a considered moral choice before acting.

In our time, the mass media consistently serve the negative form of avoidance: functioning as a denial mechanism, as a mechanism of systematic repression. We are spared ethical pain by remaining largely unconscious of what is done in our name as a nation. This, of course, is a paradox, given that the mass media are potentially tremendous tools for increasing consciousness. But obviously, it is the communal nature of that potential "knowing together" that is the threat to powerful interests behind the scenes—some of them named in this work.

This whole terrain of ethics, morality, and conscience is a tricky and dangerous minefield, especially based on practical efficiency and short-term gain. Moreover, the current backlash against so-called "political correctness" would seem to indicate a widespread reluctance to assume any kind of personal and collective accountability, a refusal of fetters freely and consciously chosen on the basis of conscience.

The Noam Chomsky Lectures opens up this terrain by revealing some of the process of "thought control," "the manufacture of consent," whereby our ethics and underlying moral basis are determined for us smoothly and effectively, and on a daily basis, by those who would profit from our collective unknowing. Thus, dissent can be seen in stark relief against that "consent" manufactured so effectively and efficiently throughout this mass-media century. It is an effort to be conscious and accountable.

I suspect Brooks and Verdecchia have taken their knocks for this work. As the reader will see, it is not "beautiful with a capital B," occasionally falls off the Universal Wit Factor Chart, delivers few yucks-per-buck, wields the Artstick with abandon, and glosses over the Freemasons. But, as a "meta-theatrical explication," it reminds us of the greater role of theatre and all art, especially the written word. As Galeano states it, "In a system of silence and fear, the power to create and to invent and to imagine attacks the rootedness of obedience." Here, Brooks and Verdecchia have imagined us, "the public," to be similarly capable.

Joyce Nelson, 1991

Production History

The Noam Chomsky Lectures was first presented as part of the Buddies in Bad Times Rhubarb! Festival at the Annex Theatre in Toronto in February 1990.

Following its run at the Annex, *The Noam Chomsky Lectures* was revised and expanded for the World Stage Festival in Toronto in June 1990, and for the Fringe of Toronto Festival in July 1990. The following text is based on a version presented during a two-week run, from March 12-31, 1991, at the Backspace, Theatre Passe Muraille. Excerpts from previous performances are included in the Notes.

The set was designed by Stephan Droege, and the production was stage-managed by Michelle Power.

All versions of the play to date have been directed and performed by the authors, Daniel Brooks and Guillermo Verdecchia.

DANIEL BROOKS *and* GUILLERMO VERDECCHIA *are seated at a table as the audience enters. The table is strewn with props and books.* BROOKS *and* VERDECCHIA *read, chat, dance, talk to people in the audience. Trini Lopez music plays. After ten or fifteen minutes, the house lights dim, and a tape is played of a Canadian Armed Forces recruitment ad. When it is over, the stage goes to black. A slide appears on a screen*

SLIDE Citizens of the democratic countries should undertake a course of intellectual self-defense to protect themselves from manipulation and control.
— Noam Chomsky, *Necessary Illusions*
SLIDE Noam Chomsky is a professor of Linguistics and Philosophy at Massachusetts Institute of Technology, fellow of the American Academy of Arts and Sciences, author of numerous books and articles on linguistics, philosophy and intellectual history, and contemporary issues.
SLIDE He's my absolute fucking favourite philosopher.
— Sky Gilbert, theatre director and playwright

Lights up

Introductions

VERDECCHIA Hello.
BROOKS Hello.
VERDECCHIA Good evening.
BROOKS Hello.
VERDECCHIA Welcome.
BROOKS Hello.
VERDECCHIA I'm Guillermo Verdecchia.
BROOKS I'm Daniel Brooks.
VERDECCHIA The pre-show music is by Trini Lopez.

BROOKS The set design is by Dora Award-winning designer Stephan Droege.[1]

VERDECCHIA I'm a Sagittarius.

BROOKS I'm a Cancer. And these are *The Noam Chomsky Lectures.*

VERDECCHIA Are there any questions? [*he waits for a response*] If there are no questions, we'll proceed.

[BROOKS *sits,* VERDECCHIA *stands*]

Clarifications

VERDECCHIA A few clarifications before we begin.

One: This is not a Wooster Group Tribute.[2]

Two: This is not a satire.

Three: Although Daniel has been to South America, and I myself was born there, we will not be performing "South American-style"[3] because, Mr. Conlogue, there is no such thing.

Four: Rumours that *The Noam Chomsky Lectures* is lip-synched are simply unfounded.

Daniel…

[VERDECCHIA *sits,* BROOKS *stands*]

BROOKS First let me state that *The Noam Chomsky Lectures* is a perpetual workshop, an unfinished play, a fourth draft, a work in progress; hence, you are a workshop audience, an unfinished audience, a fourth-draft audience, an audience in progress; hence, this is not a real play, you are not a real audience—so let's all sit back and have a whale of a good time.

Guillermo…

[BROOKS *sits,* VERDECCHIA *stands*]

VERDECCHIA Daniel and I will be making some "chaotic gestures" and using some "bizarre indigenous instruments,"[4] to borrow two phrases from *Globe and Mail* theatre critic Ray Conlogue, or as he's known in some circles...

SLIDE This show is convincing evidence of the need for an Esthetic Police.
— Ray Conlogue, *The Globe and Mail*, June 13, 1990[5]

...Constable Conlogue. One of the bizarre indigenous instruments we will be using is the Artstick. [*he holds up an elaborately decorated bamboo stick*]

SLIDE When a work resolutely refuses to view the world in anything but naïve us-versus-them terms, it is not a play but a polemic and the playwright but a pamphleteer.
— Alex Patterson, *Metropolis*, February 1, 1990

It will be used by either Daniel or myself whenever one of the performers crosses that fine line between art and demagoguery. A demonstration.

[BROOKS *stands*]

BROOKS Okay, let's talk about this Gulf War. Why didn't Bush let sanctions against Iraq work? I'll tell you why. He wanted a war, he wanted to end the talk about a peace dividend, he is seeking the legitimation of war and the elevation of the United States to the status of world mercenary policeman—
VERDECCHIA [*strikes the table with the Artstick*] The Artstick. Article 51 of *The Noam Chomsky Lectures* Charter states: "When hit with the Artstick, the speaker is effectively silenced."

[BROOKS *sits*]

VERDECCHIA I would like to draw our attention to the following:

SLIDE ...some of the fundamentals of theatre, like communication, honest emotion, engagement, and commitment to the characters on the stage.
— Robert Crew, *The Toronto Star*, June 14, 1990

These are known in some circles as "Robert's Rules." They come to us from former *Toronto Star* theatre critic Robert Crew. Now, Mr. Crew has gone on to bigger and better things, and he has left us in the very capable hands of one Geoff Chapman. More on him later. In the meantime, Robert's Rules remind us of some of the fundamentals of theatre, like honest emotion, engagement, communication, and commitment to the characters onstage. We are the characters, this is the stage. Daniel, this is particularly important for us, because we don't want *The Noam Chomsky Lectures* to turn into just another silly post-modern push-up.
Daniel...

[VERDECCHIA *sits*, BROOKS *stands*]

Terms of the Show

SLIDE The people who own the country ought to govern it.
— John Jay, first chief justice of the US Supreme Court

BROOKS These are the terms of our show: *The Noam Chomsky Lectures* is an attempt to bring to you some of the ideas present in the political writings of esteemed Professor Noam Chomsky, as well as some information you may not

14

be familiar with. According to Chomsky, you are not familiar with it because the Western Press consistently caters to the interests of Big Business, because the Western Press *is* Big Business.

Chomsky catalogues a series of coups, invasions, and mass murders by countless Third World governments, all supported by the American government, and, in turn, by we Canadians through our quiet, and in a more recent case, not so quiet, acquiescence. The Americans support these violent regimes mainly because they support the business interests of companies such as: The United Fruit Company, IT&T, Pepsi-Cola, Coca-Cola, General Motors and General Electric, which, by the way, owns the National Broadcasting Corporation, is heavily involved in the arms industry and the nuclear industry, and is a former employer of Ronald Reagan.[6] You can bet that when a populist government in a Third World country begins to nationalize industry, allow labour organizations, redistribute land, and control the flight of profit and petrodollars from that country, an American-backed coup will not be far behind. Since the American military can no longer police the entire world by themselves, they support certain other military governments to be, as Richard Nixon put it, "cops on the beat."

Chomsky shows how the Western Press practises self-censorship and caters to the ideological line of Big Business and government by giving weight to certain stories...

[VERDECCHIA *holds up a full-page newspaper article about Ivana Trump*]

...while ignoring others.

[*Using tweezers,* VERDECCHIA *displays a two-inch article about casualties in Panama*]

15

In a democratic society, where there is no explicit censorship, there is a need to control thought through what the democratic theorist Walter Lippman once called "the manufacture of consent." The media is Big Business and serves as a conduit for the messages of advertisers—more Big Business. The owners of the media and the owners of the corporations they advertise for are members of the same country clubs, sit in the same corporate boardrooms, and sit in the same steam baths. The writers, newscasters and editors know where their paycheques are coming from. There are real-world pressures on all of us. For example, it would be reckless of me to publicly attack *Toronto Star* theatre critic Geoff Chapman. I am the co-director of a small theatre company, and it might come back at me...but what the fuck.

SLIDE Photo of Geoff Chapman

Mirror Game is a play recently presented at Young People's Theatre in Toronto. It examines physical and psychological abuse, and how abusive behaviour can be passed from parent to child, in a kind of mirror game. The play gives teenagers tools to recognize patterns of abuse, and urges them to say no to abuse, to break the cycle of violence, to break the mirror, as it were. In the play, the parents are portrayed as broad caricatures, not unlike the parents in a *Peanuts* cartoon or the caricatures of women in the sex farces Mr. Chapman seems to like so much. Chapman took offence. In his review of the play, he wrote that parents are just a "new trendy target" of the "Nazi-spirited regulators who want to control Canadian lives, Canadian thinking." Nazi-spirited regulators indeed. His list of old and no-longer trendy targets of the Nazi-spirited down at Young People's Theatre includes: Tory finance ministers, people who smoke cigars (of which he is one), and the Ku Klux Klan, "all fifty of them." Hmmm. Perhaps Mr. Chapman is unaware of the flourishing of neo-Nazi and white supremacist groups throughout the world. Also on his list of no longer trendy targets: the military-industrial complex.

VERDECCHIA & BROOKS Ha!

BROOKS Well, Mr. Chapman, perhaps you're not aware that between 50 and 65 percent of every US tax dollar goes to the military-industrial complex—some of that money goes to make things that kill people. Finally on his list of unimportant targets: people who let pets poop prolifically. Well, ladies and gentlemen, poop on this...[7]

We of *The Noam Chomsky Lectures* are concerned with the control that Big Business has on the formation and dissemination of information, we are concerned with our own collective moral hypocrisy and cowardice, and we are concerned with the movement in theatre towards a greater and greater focus on market forces. We are concerned with the predictable consequences.

[*Pause*]

Are there any questions or comments?

VERDECCHIA I have two comments, Daniel. If I may...

BROOKS Certainly, Guillermo.

[**BROOKS** *sits*, **VERDECCHIA** *stands*]

VERDECCHIA First, it has been suggested to us that criticizing Geoff Chapman is like shooting fish in a barrel. Tonight's special is...fish in a barrel.

Second. Daniel has just spoken of some of the connections that exist between the corporate elite and the mass media and we would like to assure you, the members of our audience, that we are not conspiracy-mongers—

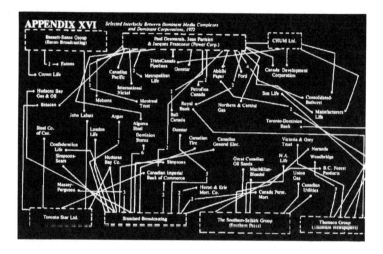

—and draw your attention to this flow chart from 1972, which shows some selected linkages between the boards of major corporations and media complexes. [*he points out the following connections on the chart*]

Here we have Standard Broadcasting, which owns a number of radio stations, among other things. The president of Standard Broadcasting is also a director for the Canadian Imperial Bank of Commerce, or CIBC, which we can see is also connected to Power Corporation and *The Toronto Star*. The CIBC also has connections to the local theatre community. The Canadian Stage Company (Toronto's largest not-for-profit theatre) pays some three hundred thousand dollars annually to the CIBC in interest payments alone. The CIBC also holds part of the mortgage for this building—that's Theatre Passe Muraille—and the CIBC is the official bank of *The Noam Chomsky Lectures*. The CIBC recently pulled some advertising from a CBC television programme because of some pressure from the British Columbia Forest Industry. A spokesperson for the CIBC explained that they were sensitive to the concerns of their business clients. Daniel, perhaps you and I can exert some pressure on the CIBC by threatening to withdraw the remaining $47.26 from *The Noam Chomsky Lectures* account.

To return to the chart: the president of Standard Broadcasting is also a director of Argus Corporation, which holds the controlling interest in Standard Broadcasting. Are you following this? Argus is owned by one Conrad Black who owns, among many other things, Hollinger Corporation. Hollinger Corporation, among many, many other things, owns *The Jerusalem Post*. *The Jerusalem Post* would show up on a chart in a different country. One of the directors of Hollinger Corporation is former Canadian ambassador to the United States, one of the "architects of Free Trade," and head of the Canada Council, Mr. Allan Gotlieb. Interestingly enough, Mr. Gotlieb, head of the largest public-sector funding body for the arts in Canada, is also director of an American publishing firm, MacMillan Inc. Hmm. Also a director of Hollinger is former American Secretary of State Henry Kissinger. Hmm hmm.

Now, over here is the Thomson Group, which owns any number of things, among them Thomson Newspapers, which controls some forty dailies, including the lovely *Globe and Mail.* Thomson is a very large chain, they are very big in the States as well, and they are constantly expanding, snapping up newspapers. Buying newspapers means dealing with the banks. Thomson, then, is fortunate that their president and chairman, Ken Thomson (one of the richest men in the world), is also director for the Toronto Dominion Bank. Lord Thomson, his daddy, was a director of the Royal Bank, which we can see is plugged into Power Corporation. And the executive vice-president of Thomson, a former minister of citizenship and finance, is chairman of Victoria & Grey Trust. Obviously, these connections make getting a loan that much easier for Thomson. I'd also like to point out that Ken Thomson, chairman and president of Thomson Newspapers (and one of the richest men in the world) is also a director of Abitibi Paper, which we can see is plugged into Power Corporation. This is a helpful connection: Abitibi makes paper and Thomson Newspapers, hey, they use paper.

Finally, I'd like to point out that Ken Thomson, president and chairman of Thomson Newspapers (and one of the richest men in the world), attended Upper Canada College, as did my good friend and co-worker, Daniel Brooks.

[**BROOKS** *looks at audience, pauses, then looks back at* **VERDECCHIA**]

Daniel Brooks is a director of an obscure Kensington Market theatre company...they're not on this chart.

In the past twenty years, there has been a flurry of buyouts and mergers, and media ownership has become intensely concentrated, and if we were to have a flow chart representing the links between media complexes and corporations for 1991, it might look something like this:

SLIDE MEDIA connected to CORPORATIONS

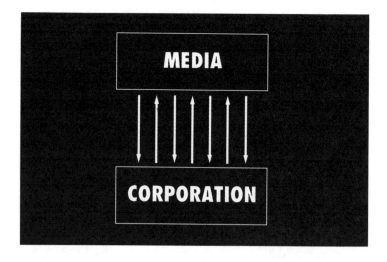

Here we have the Media bloc and here the Corporate bloc, the arrows indicating a kind of dynamic relationship between the two blocs. A deep interpenetration, if you will. Finally, I think it would be safe to say that all of the people on this chart and all of the people on the previous chart support Free Trade.[9]

[VERDECCHIA *sits*]

History

[BROOKS *and* VERDECCHIA *stand*]

BROOKS We would now like to present a brief, and by no means exhaustive, history of Latin America in this century.

VERDECCHIA 1904: US troops land in Honduras for the first of five times in the next twenty years.

BROOKS 1908: US troops land in Panama for the first of four times in the next decade.

VERDECCHIA 1909: The American secretary of state, Philander Knox, is also a shareholder in and lawyer for the R&L Mine Company. Nicaraguan President Zelaya insists that the R&L Mine Company pay taxes. The US invades Nicaragua and President Zelaya is replaced with the R&L Mine Company's accountant.

BROOKS 1921: US pressures Guatemala to overthrow its president—enabling the United Fruit Company to expand and ripen.

VERDECCHIA 1930: With American assistance, the dictator, Trujillo, takes over in the Dominican Republic.

BROOKS 1932: US warships (and three Canadian warships) stand by as 2 percent of the El Salvadorean population is massacred.

VERDECCHIA 1948: First US military training mission is sent to El Salvador.

BROOKS 1954: Guatemalan President Arbenz seizes uncultivated United Fruit Company land and offers to pay the United Fruit Company what the company claims the land is worth. An invasion to overthrow President Arbenz is planned. Planners of the invasion include: John Dulles, American secretary of state, lawyer for the United Fruit Company, and brother to the head of the CIA; Walter Smith, under secretary of state and future board member of the United Fruit Company; Robert Hill, ambassador to Guatemala and future board member of the United Fruit Company; John Cabot, secretary of state for inter American affairs and brother to the president of the United Fruit Company. President Arbenz is overthrown and a *Time* magazine journalist is given the job of framing Guatemala's new constitution.

VERDECCHIA 1960: President Kennedy authorizes the invasion of Cuba. This invasion, known as the Bay of Pigs, is launched from Nicaragua, Guatemala, and Miami.

BROOKS 1964: Brazilian President Goulard has introduced agrarian reform and nationalized the oil industry. With American assistance, he is overthrown.

VERDECCHIA 1966: US forces participate in Operation Guatemala. Eight thousand are killed. Among those killed are Indians, peasants, guerrillas, academics, and labour leaders.

BROOKS 1973: In Chile, the democratically-elected Marxist government of Salvador Allende is, with much American assistance, overthrown.

VERDECCHIA 1981: US begins a proxy war on Nicaragua.

BROOKS 1983: US invades Grenada.

VERDECCHIA 1989: US invades Panama.

A Play Within the Play

VERDECCHIA We would now like to present a meeting between a group of American senators and Iraqi President
Saddam Hussein. This meeting took place on April 12,
1990. Daniel will play all the senators.

[BROOKS *dons a large Uncle Sam hat*]

He's the one wearing the big hat. He will wear hat number
one for Senator Number One, and hat two

[BROOKS *shows a second hat, identical to the first hat*]

for Senator Two. He will speak with a cheesy Southern
accent for both senators. I will play Hussein, wear a military hat, and use a cheesy pan-Arab accent. At the risk of
offending *Toronto Star* theatre critic Geoff Chapman, the
senators and Hussein will be played as broad caricatures.
This scene is based on a word-for-word transcript.[10]

[*Abrupt lighting change*]

SENATOR ONE I enjoy meeting candid and open people. This is a trademark
of those of us who live in the "Wild West." ... One of the reasons that
we telephoned President Bush yesterday evening was to tell the president that our visit to Iraq would cost us a great deal of popularity, and
that many people would attack us for coming to Iraq.... But President
Bush said, "Go there. I want you there.... If you are criticized because
of your visit to Iraq, I will defend you and speak on your behalf." The
things that you just talked about [regarding Israeli military power] are
the same things we once talked about in the US regarding the Soviet
Union. Who will strike the other first; who will push the button
first.... [But now] Secretary of State Baker and Foreign Minister
Shevardnadze have become friends, and they go fishing together in the

river…. Democracy is a very confusing issue. I believe that your problems lie with the Western media and not with the US government. …what I advise is that you invite them to come here and see for themselves.

HUSSEIN They are welcome. We hope that they will come to see Iraq and, after they do, write whatever they like….

SENATOR TWO I did have some reservations on whether I should come on this visit.

HUSSEIN You certainly will not regret it afterward.

SENATOR TWO I do not regret it, Mr. President. I am not the right person to be your public-relations man, but allow me to suggest a few things…. …I have been sitting here and listening to you for about an hour, and I am now aware that you are a strong and intelligent man and that you want peace. … I believe Mr. President, that you can be a very influential force for peace in the Middle East. But, as I said, I am not your public-relations man.

[Lights abruptly return to previous state. End of the play within the play]

VERDECCHIA Daniel and I will be taking donations for the Saddam Hussein Public Relations Fund. Please place your contributions in the big hat.

[BROOKS *places one of the Uncle Sam hats downstage*]

As I said, this scene is based on a word-for-word transcript of a meeting which took place on April 12, 1990, at a time when the American government was actively courting the Iraqi government. In fact, it was in the month of April that the assistant secretary of state for the Middle East testified in Congress that the United States had no responsibility, no commitment, to defend Kuwait. There was a time when Saddam Hussein was our friend, as was Nicolae Ceausescu, as was Manuel Noriega.

History, Part Two

BROOKS We will now present a brief, and by no means exhaustive, history of the Middle East in this century.

VERDECCHIA 1917: The Balfour Declaration commits Britain to the establishment of a Jewish homeland in Palestine. Most of the population at the time is Arab.

BROOKS 1936 to 1939: Palestinian Arabs revolt against the British. The revolt is crushed with considerable brutality.

VERDECCHIA 1947: The UN General Assembly recommends the partition of Palestine into a Jewish and a Palestinian State. The Arab population rejects this recommendation. Civil strife breaks out, with atrocities committed by both Arabs and Jews.

BROOKS 1948: The state of Israel is founded. The armies of the Arab nations attack Israel. The war ends with half of the proposed Palestinian state being incorporated by Israel, the other half by Trans-Jordan, now Jordan. Approximately 700 thousand Arabs either flee or are expelled from the area.

VERDECCHIA 1953: The Iranian government nationalizes the oil industry. With American assistance, this government is overthrown and the pro-Western dictator, the Shah, is installed in power.

BROOKS 1956: Egyptian President Nassar nationalizes the Suez Canal. The forces of Israel, Britain, and France attack Egypt.

VERDECCHIA 1967: Israel attacks Egypt. By the end of the Six Day War, Israel has conquered the land known today as the Occupied Territories and the Sinai Peninsula.

BROOKS 1973: Egypt and Syria attack Israel. Most of the fighting occurs in the Occupied Territories.

VERDECCHIA 1978: Israel attacks South Lebanon. Two thousand Palestinians and Lebanese are killed, two hundred and fifty thousand are made refugees.

BROOKS 1980: Iraq invades Iran. The United States and other Western powers supply arms and intelligence services to both sides. The war lasts eight years, and over one million people are left dead.

VERDECCHIA 1982: Israel invades Lebanon. Approximately twenty thousand Palestinians and Lebanese are killed, countless others are imprisoned or made refugees.

BROOKS 1987: The Palestinian uprising in the Occupied Territories begins. The violence continues to this day.

VERDECCHIA 1990: Iraq invades Kuwait.

BROOKS 1991: The American-led coalition forces begin the Gulf War. By war's end, approximately 100 thousand Iraqis are dead.[11]

VERDECCHIA 1991: *The Noam Chomsky Lectures* is presented in the Backspace at Theatre Passe Muraille.

Universal Wit Factor

SLIDE Universal Wit Factor Chart for *The Noam Chomsky Lectures*

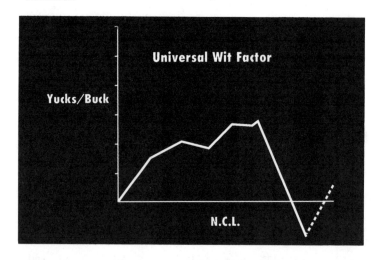

VERDECCHIA And now I'd like to draw your attention to this

26

graph which shows the Universal Wit Factor or UWF over the course of *The Noam Chomsky Lectures*. The concept of the Universal Wit Factor, or "Oof," was inspired by Geoff Chapman, jazz and theatre reviewer for *The Toronto Star*. It's measured in a yucks-per-buck quotient, and it's a radical new standard for measuring the worth of any theatrical presentation. Basically it works like this: when the Wit Factor is high, when yer getting plenty of yucks-per-buck, then that's good. When you're not, well, then you're getting ripped off.

Let's take a closer look at the chart, shall we? [*with a pointer in hand, he moves towards the graph*] Here we have the vertical axis showing the yucks-per-buck quotient, and here the horizontal axis showing *The Noam Chomsky Lectures* travelling through space and time that way. It starts off at zero, picks up with a couple of good witty remarks, has a couple of peaks, and then there's a dip. Perhaps a bit too much information, or as Jill Lawless of *NOW* magazine might say, this is an area where our "reach exceeds [our] grasp."[12] Little peak here, very consistent, when Daniel says, "What the fuck," and we click to the picture of Geoff Chapman. And of course, this peak here, which is the moment we've arrived at now, when we do something like this.

VERDECCHIA & BROOKS "We are morons, tried and true! And we'll do our yell for you—Oooga Booga Booga Blahhhh, Chomsky Chomsky eat 'em raw."

[*Pause*]

VERDECCHIA Well, our audience usually laughs. Of course, you are a particularly sophisticated audience. We are now actually in this period of steep decline. We've gone below the level of the graph, and we hope eventually to come out on the other side. What I'd like to suggest is that we take a break to compose ourselves, because we are going into some difficult material. There are going to be few yucks for your buck, so let's take a break, concentrate, and prepare for the difficult material which lies ahead. Let's take five to revive.

Intermission

House lights come up, and Lopez' "Lemon Tree" begins to play. Twelve seconds go by. Obnoxious noise

VERDECCHIA Okay, break's over.

House lights out

Lecture

VERDECCHIA An article in the February 25 edition of *Maclean's* magazine describes the trials of the present Canadian government as they try to "sell [the Gulf] war to a nation of peacekeepers." This article explains that Canada's position is a difficult one, complicated by the "conflicting Canadian traditions of peacekeeping and participation in Western military alliances." A March 4 article in *Maclean's* explains that even though Canada took an offensive role in the war in the Gulf, that our participation in the coalition would "not rule out taking part in a peacekeeping force." An expert cited in this article explains that our reputation as a peacekeeper is still very strong. Our reputation as a peacekeeper, as a nation of quiet diplomats, is consistently reinforced by our mainstream press, and by our political leaders. Lucien Bouchard, leader of the Bloc Québécois speaking on the Gulf War, said, "the government has distanced itself from the wisest, the most noble, and the greatest of Canadian traditions, which is above all, to seek peace." And a February 11 article in *The Globe and Mail* asks, "does Canadian involvement in the war in the Persian Gulf mean that Canada has turned its back on its tradition as an international peacekeeper?" We will now examine three historical examples that challenge the notion that Canada is, in fact, a nation of peacekeepers.

SLIDE Vietnam

Vietnam. In 1954, French troops pulled out of Vietnam under the terms laid out in the Geneva Peace Accords. The accords called for a cease-fire, the withdrawal of all foreign personnel and bases. It also called for the reunification of Vietnam through an election to be held in 1956. Fearful that the Vietnamese populace would vote overwhelmingly for a Communist government, the US took steps to ensure that the elections never took place. They introduced fresh troops and launched a brutal war of aggression (which included the use of chemical weapons) against a peasant society. During this time, Canada was one of three members on the International Control Commission (ICC) which was established under the Geneva Accords to oversee the accords and keep the peace. Canada used its position on the ICC to provide a cover for American activities: providing propaganda in the guise of neutral reports, whitewashing the regime in Saigon, accusing the North Vietnamese of aggression which never occurred, and acting as messengers and information gatherers for the US administration.

SLIDE Aggression is aggression whether it takes place in Europe, Ethiopia, or Vietnam.
— Paul Martin, external affairs secretary, 1965

Canadian politicians were generally supportive of the American war. They supported it, as Canadians usually do, by echoing American justifications. [*he refers to the slide*] We also supported the war effort by providing aid to South Vietnam only, thus freeing up South Vietnamese resources for more war spending, and by testing Toxic Agents Orange, Blue, and Purple in New Brunswick before they were used on live Vietnamese people in the South East Asian jungles.

Successive Conservative and Liberal governments tried to maintain that Canada was not directly involved in the war. Nobel Peace Prize winner Lester Pearson pointed out that, "The shipment of Canadian military supplies to Vietnam would be incompatible with our role in the International Control Commission."

SLIDE The shipment of Canadian military supplies would be incompatible with our role in the International Control Commission.
— Prime Minister Lester Pearson, 1965

Peacekeeper Pearson was engaged in some semantic hair-splitting here. No, Canada did not send arms directly to Vietnam, but we did sell them to the US, and what the Americans then did with them was not Ottawa's concern. Recently released cabinet documents reveal that cabinet was well aware that the US Department of Defense had increased its procurement of a number of items bound for use in Vietnam. In fact, Canadian governments encouraged the procurement of Canadian arms through a number of grant programmes designed to assist Canadian weapons manufacturers.

SLIDE It's all very well to talk about Vietnam, but what about Canada? Canada has an economic life to lead.
— Paul Martin, external affairs secretary, 1967

Of the $2.5 billion of war material which Canada sold to the US between 1965 and 1973, approximately forty percent consisted of materials bound directly for Vietnam. We provided everything from aircraft to bomb bays to grenades to napalm to rye whiskey. The bullets used in the Mai Lai Massacre were made in Canada.

The American war on Vietnam left over 1.7 million people dead, wounded over 2 million and made several million refugees.[13] It also made Canada the largest per capita military exporter in the world.[14]

SLIDE We were against the war as everyone knows.
— Paul Martin, external affairs secretary, 1973

SLIDE Indonesia

In 1975, Indonesia invaded the former Portuguese colony of East Timor. Since then 250 thousand people have died as a result of starvation and indiscriminate slaughter by the Indonesian army. Canada has supported this slaughter through diplomatic channels, by selling arms to Indonesia, and through bilateral aid—that's government-to-government aid. In the UN, Canada has consistently refused to support resolutions calling for the withdrawal of occupation troops. In fact, a spokesperson for the Department of External Affairs has said that Canada recognizes Indonesian sovereignty in East Timor. Our sale of arms to the rampaging Indonesian military directly contradicts the Export/Import Act which states: "Canada will closely control the export of military goods to countries engaged in hostilities."

SLIDE Canada will closely control the export of military goods to countries engaged in hostilities.
— Export/Import Act

Indonesia, busy slaughtering a quarter-million people, was clearly engaged in a hostility. Indonesia, with over three hundred Canadian companies operating in it, has also been made a core recipient of development assistance. Since 1971, Indonesia has received over $700 million of Canadian aid. According to *The Globe and Mail,* Canadian aid "is quietly spent on mostly laudatory projects and humane programmes among people who desperately need our help." That aid money is quietly spent is incontestable.

SLIDE South Africa

For several decades now, the inhuman apartheid system of South Africa, modelled in part on Canada's own system of reserves, has terrorized, tortured, and murdered the non-white population of South Africa. Recent media coverage of the changes taking place in that country give the impression that Canada was at the forefront of the international anti-apartheid movement. Jeffrey Simpson, of *The Globe and Mail,* in June 1990 applauded "the policy of successive Canadian governments to oppose apartheid and to administer such economic and political sanctions as could be agreed upon within the Commonwealth." Returning to reality,[15] we will discover that for almost thirty years, Canadian governments did nothing concrete or effective in the fight against apartheid.

The same Trudeau government that called for "a positive and vigorous approach to human rights" approved all International Monetary Fund loans to South Africa. In the UN, Canada opposed proposals for an oil embargo and for a conference on sanctions, and abstained on proposals to end military and nuclear collaboration. In 1978, we introduced a voluntary code of conduct for Canadian businesses operating in South Africa, but the Canadian Export Development Corporation, which is a government agency, continued to use its corporate account to promote trade with South Africa until 1982. We also allowed the sale of military technology in spite of a mandatory UN arms embargo.

It was not until 1986, when leading African and Asian members of the Commonwealth threatened to withdraw from the association, that Canada took any effective measures. It was the threat posed to Canada's relationship with the Commonwealth, and not any professed concern for human rights, that finally motivated the Mulroney government to move against the apartheid regime.

[*Slide screen goes blank*]

This overview is by no means exhaustive. Only a lack of time prevents us from examining Canada's ongoing relationships with Bangladesh, Chile, Ecuador, Egypt, Guatemala, Israel, India, Kenya, Morocco, Mexico, Peru, Philippines, Sri Lanka, Turkey, and Zaire.

These are all countries with a long history of official violence against their citizens, or countries engaged in hostilities, countries that Canada trades with, countries that Canada gives official development assistance to, countries that Canada grants export permits for arms to.

The examples cited here as well as the recent activities of our government reveal that the real Canadian traditions are quiet complicity and hypocritical moral posturing. This nation of quiet diplomats, of peacekeepers, is in fact a nation of quiet profiteers, a nation that has enriched itself on the misery and destruction of millions of lives all over the globe.

[*Silence*]

Because we live in a democratic society, the information we have presented is available if one knows where to

33

look, how to piece it together, and, most importantly, if one has the time to do so. The information does not appear in our mainstream press because of a combination of factors: pressures from advertisers, editorial pressures, inadequate information or directed misinformation from government sources, and the built-in ideological assumptions of the journalists themselves. These factors all contribute to historical engineering, or the manufacture of consent.

[**BROOKS** *rings a bell*][16]

Manufacturing Consent

BROOKS [*holds up a copy of the book* Manufacturing Consent]
Manufacturing Consent is a book co-authored by Noam Chomsky and Edward S. Herman. It is an in-depth analysis of how the media shapes the news and how it sets the political agenda. In the following minutes, we will give examples of how the media sets the agenda, and for each example we will give a theatrical demonstration—this is the theatre after all.

One: Choice of Topic. Example.

Manuel Noriega's lifestyle was a favourite choice of topic both during and after the American invasion of Panama. This from *The Los Angeles Times*: "Vats of blood. Animal entrails. A picture of Adolf Hitler. Spike-heeled shoes. More than 100 pounds of cocaine. All were part of the bizarre scenes encountered by American troops as they stormed the inner sanctum of deposed Panamanian strongman Manuel Noriega."

Not chosen as a topic was the fact that the invasion was, according to American law, illegal, as only Congress, and not the president, can constitutionally declare war. The press has also chosen to turn a blind eye to Bush's own lifestyle. [*he puts the microphone to the side and leans towards the audience*] Rumours that the press would report on Bush's extra-marital activities during the 1988 election campaign caused a plunge in the stock market. The gossip never hit the press. [*he leans even farther over the table and speaks in a whisper*] Also not a choice of topic—and I hope this goes no farther than this room—is the drinking habit of our own prime minister.[17]

Demonstration of Choice of Topic.

Guillermo?

VERDECCHIA Yes?

BROOKS Do you do drugs?

VERDECCHIA Well…yes.

BROOKS Did you do drugs or have a drink at any time during the creation of this show?

VERDECCHIA I might have had an Armagnac…

BROOKS How many women have you slept with in your lifetime Guillermo?

VERDECCHIA I don't know Daniel—

BROOKS Give us a round number.

VERDECCHIA I don't keep track—

BROOKS Round it off to the nearest ten.

VERDECCHIA Daniel—

BROOKS Guillermo, did you not tell me on August 18, 1989, and I quote, "I will never work with Crow's Theatre again." And then on January 22 of this year, did you not say, and I quote, "I got a part in Crow's new play, and I'm gonna take it."

VERDECCHIA Well, yes—

BROOKS Yes, you did.

And on March 5, 1991, when you were asked to respond to an Ontario Arts Council survey that was asking theatre artists how the Ontario Arts Council could better serve the artist, did you not say, you who are a theatre artist…you are a theatre artist, are you not?

VERDECCHIA Yes, I am.

BROOKS Yes, you are. Did you not say to me, and I quote, "I'm a very busy person, I don't consult for free."

VERDECCHIA Daniel, that was a—

BROOKS [*screaming*] Did you or didn't you? [*pause, then calmly*] You did. And when I asked you whether or not you would be willing to do an extra, non-paying performance of *The Noam Chomsky Lectures* at DuMaurier World Stage down at Harbourfront, did you not say, and I quote, "Not for what they're paying us."

No, Mister Ver*decchia*, the issue here has nothing to do with your paranoid ideas about thought control in a democratic society and *everything* to do with your tendency towards alcoholism, womanizing, greed, and gross hypocrisy! [*silence*] I see that Guillermo is experiencing some of the same emotions that his character is going through at the present time.[18]

Two: Placement. Example.

SLIDE A two-page spread from *The Toronto Star*, with a full-page ad for a large retail chain

Behind me you see pages eight and nine of *The Toronto Star*. Somewhere up there is an article that refers to the claim that the US government has illegally hidden thousands of secret intelligence documents from the lawyers of ousted Panamanian dictator Manuel Noriega. In other words, they've broken the law in a very big and very bad way. Would you like to show us where this article is placed, Guillermo?

[VERDECCHIA *indicates a tiny five-centimetre column at the very bottom of the page*]

Demonstration of Placement.

Guillermo will now place his head inside that trash can and give his views on the American invasion of Panama, while I babble on about nothing in particular.

VERDECCHIA [*puts the trash can on his head*] The American invasion of Panama clearly violates International Law as well as the American Constitution because George Bush did not consult Congress. It's really interesting to look at the statistics on this one: I think that the American Congress has declared war something like 5 times while the president has led the country into war something like 135 times. We should also bear in mind that this adventurist escapade killed approximately one thousand Panamanians. We might also note that this little victory in the War on Drugs confiscated exactly zero grams of illegal substances. This action should be recognized as yet another vile instance of intervention and neo-imperialism. Let's look at the history of Panama, the Canal, and Panamanian racial structures and class structures in order to get a better idea of what the invasion was really about...

BROOKS [*referring to an ad that dominates the page*] "Holt Renfrew's semi-annual store-wide sale starts today!" This was months ago, so I wouldn't go down there if I were you. The sale is off and you would be wasting your time. I have a question though. Question: Is Holt Renfrew experiencing the same problems that Creeds experienced some months ago? [*pause*] No? [*pause*] Nobody here in the retail business? I hear it is really bad, it's really rough out there. I have a theory as to why the retail business is in such rough shape. Anyone care to hear it? [*pause*] No? [*pause*] Yes? Well, because we no longer care about quality. There is no quality control in our lives, we are not discerning. We want more—bigger, faster, higher, buy it, eat it, fuck it—but we don't care about quality, refinement. For Christ's fucking sake, look at these books here, we could at least have placed them with the spine towards you so you could see the titles,

look at this anti-theatre mess on this table, this cheap
plastic bell that we only use *twice* in the show and for no
goddamn reason, we might as well just...just...look. Look
at this shit. Everything is made of plastic, cheap fucking
plastic. This [*refers to the plastic pointer*]...this [*he hits the
desk with the pointer*]...this shit here...by the way, who do
you like more, Guillermo or I...

[*He hits the plastic trash can that rests on* VERDECCHIA*'s head*]

Thank you, Guillermo.

[VERDECCHIA *removes the garbage can from his head and spits a
ball of paper out of his mouth*]

Three: Ideological Assumptions. Example.
We are actually concerned with democracy in Latin
America and the Middle East when all evidence argues
against it.
The following is from a *Globe and Mail* editorial *con-
demning* the American invasion of Panama. "Extremism in
the defence of democracy is still extremism." The assumption here is that the invasion had anything whatsoever to
do with the defence of democracy.
Demonstration of Ideological Assumption.
We, the actors, will assume that you, the audience, will
assume that we, the actors, won't throw anything at you or
squirt water at you when we turn off the lights in the
auditorium. Lights, please.

[*Lights go out.* BROOKS *and* VERDECCHIA *throw paper balls and
squirt water at the audience*]

Thank you.

[Lights rise]

Four: Blind Stupidity. Example.

Efrain Rios Montt is a former Guatemalan dictator responsible for the murder of countless Guatemalan civilians. This from the July 1, 1990 issue of *The Toronto Star.* "Many Guatemalans believe what happened was necessary. During [Montt's] rule, relative safety returned to the streets, and corruption dropped dramatically." The suggestion that a government murdering its citizens brings safety to the streets, and that a government murdering its citizens is anything but the height of corruption, is blindly stupid. I hope this stupidity is evident to us all.

Demonstration of Blind Stupidity.

Guillermo...

VERDECCHIA Uh...I'm glad you asked that, Daniel, because you know a lot of people ask me about it. [*his elbows slip off the table edge*] Gee, this table is very slippery. It gives me an opportunity to discuss one of my favourite subjects—[*he stands, with his foot in a bucket*] Freemasons. You know they've got secret handshakes, [*he moves from behind the desk, revealing that his fly is undone and his shirt-tail is protruding*] they know who they are, but we don't know who they are. Not much we can do about Freemasons, so kick back, live a little, think good thoughts, and never trespass at the African Lion Safari. [*he does a pratfall*]

BROOKS Thank you, Guillermo.

Five: Biased Sources. Example.

The Pentagon has an information service that employs thousands of people and spends hundreds of millions of dollars a year. Journalists use this biased source of information. It gives them stories, saves them time, and helps them meet deadlines.

Demonstration of Biased Sources.

As we of *The Noam Chomsky Lectures* did not have time to consult the Pentagon as to what they did or did not think about our humble little show, Guillermo will now give a brief review of *The Noam Chomsky Lectures*.

VERDECCHIA [*reading*] *The Noam Chomsky Lectures* is a breathtaking work of indescribable Beauty with a capital *B*. Immaculately conceived and rigorously constructed, it deconstructs deconstruction and restructures itself into a construct of considerable structure. Daniel Brooks and Guillermo Verdecchia are consummate performers. The haircuts are exquisite, the costumes resplendent. The casually elegant design by Dora Award winner Stephan Droege is a magnificent triumph of proto-neo-crypto Italian minimalism. And then it goes on to rave about the writing, something about Shakespeare, and Zola.

BROOKS Six: Quoting Out of Context. Example.

On the back cover of Noam Chomsky's book about the Middle East, *The Fateful Triangle*, the publishers, Black Rose Books, have chosen to cite *The New York Times Book Review*, and I quote, "Judged in terms of the power, range, novelty, and influence of his thought, Noam Chomsky is arguably the most important intellectual alive." Strangely, Black Rose neglects to include another sentence from the review, which states that Chomsky talks "pure nonsense" about history.[19]

Demonstration of Quoting Out of Context.

I will now quote *Globe and Mail* theatre critic Ray Conlogue out of context, and make it appear as though he were calling himself a five-year-old child.

In his review of local clown act Mump and Smoot, he writes: "*Caged*, the new show by Mump and Smoot, marks the second time I have seen these urban clowns perform, and I still don't get it." Later in the review, he writes: "There is nothing in their shows that cannot be understood by a six-year-old."

Seven: The Memory Hole. Example.

In 1973, the democratically-elected Marxist government of Salvador Allende was overthrown. The leader of the junta—that was in part orchestrated by Henry Kissinger—was Augusto Pinochet, a bad man who ruled Chile for sixteen and a half years with a brutal hand. He was responsible for the deaths of thousands of people, the torture of countless others, and the exile of many more, some of whom came to our fair city by the lake.

Between March 9 and March 16 of last year, Paul Knox of *The Globe and Mail* wrote four articles about the return to democracy in Chile. He wrote, "Thousands of Canadians abstained from Chile's noble red wines and bargain whites during [General] Pinochet's sixteen and a half year rule…. Some…pressed the Canadian government to take a strong stand against the regime." What he doesn't mention is that Canadian aid to Chile actually increased during Pinochet's rule. Nor does Knox mention the involvement of the CIA in the overthrow of the Allende government. Without the generous support of the Americans, Knox would not be writing about the return to democracy in Chile, because democracy would never have left the country in the first place. Nevertheless, the American engineering of the coup has been dropped into *The Globe and Mail*'s Memory Hole.

Demonstration of Memory Hole.

[*Silence.* BROOKS *and* VERDECCHIA *stare blankly at the audience. After some time,* BROOKS *hesitantly consults his notes, finds his place, and continues*]

Eight: Captions and Headlines. Example.

I have here an article from the May 7, 1989 issue of *The Toronto Star.* [*he holds up the front page of the "World News" section*]

The headline reads, "Arafat offers a 'peaceful' face." Note the "peaceful" is in quotation marks, the implication being that he's a two-faced lying snit. Perhaps he is. He is a politician after all.

This article is about what *The Toronto Star* refers to as Arafat's 1989 "peace offensive." In 1989 Arafat toured Europe and North Africa, and made a series of statements that called for the renunciation of terrorism, that called for the recognition of the State of Israel, and even called for the establishment of a UN security buffer zone on the Palestinian side of any proposed Palestinian-Israeli border.

The subheading reads, "His recent declarations are radical moves for PLO." This is entirely misleading. Ever since the mid-seventies, the PLO has been moderating its stance toward Israel. In 1976, the PLO supported a UN Security Council resolution that called for the recognition of Israel and called for peace and security for all states in the region. This resolution, which had broad support in the international community, was vetoed by the United States and rejected by Israel. Throughout the eighties, Arafat made a series of statements calling for negotiations with Israel. The negotiations were to lead to mutual recognition between the PLO and Israel. Israel refused to talk. We do not have the time to go into questioning the PLO's sincerity. Neither do we have time to discuss why Israel is not interested in talking peace with the PLO.

What we do know is that there are many powerful members of the Israeli Parliament who want to hang on to the Occupied Territories. They want to keep the land. They want a greater Israel, just as Syria wants a greater Syria, just as Daniel Brooks wants a greater apartment. [*he holds up the article*]

The photo of Arafat's "peaceful face" is accompanied by a caption that reads: "Yasser Arafat: series of declarations in recent months have alienated the chairman from some top PLO officials." This caption sheds doubt on Arafat's authority, and draws our attention to dissent within the PLO. Now, certainly the dissent exists. It also exists within the Israeli parliament, and it exists within our own government. You may remember the goings-on in the Senate not too long ago. The caption could just as well have read: "Israel not interested in Arafat peace proposals."

SLIDE Israel isn't interested in any peace initiatives at this time.
— Yitzhak Shamir, February 15, 1991

SLIDE Israel will stand up against strong diplomatic attacks.
— Yitzhak Shamir, February 27, 1991

Demonstration of Captions and Headlines.
Here is a photo of Guillermo and me.

SLIDE Photo of Brooks and Verdecchia

And the caption.

SLIDE "Writers" Guillermo Verdecchia and Daniel Brooks prepare their play *The Noam Chomsky Lectures*, a polemic in support of international terrorism.

This is, of course, a demonstration. Guillermo and I do not support terrorism of any kind, but if you wish to discredit us, here is your opportunity to quote us out of context.

Nine: Doublespeak. Example.

The media uses certain words to convey an ideology rather than to express the truth. "Terrorism" is such a word. "Terrorism" refers to acts of violence by others against Western powers. Acts of violence by Western powers or by groups supported by Western powers, by "proxies" such as the contras or the El Salvadorean government, are never referred to as "terrorism." They are referred to as "counter-insurgency," "acts of self-defence," "freedom fighting," "pre-emptive strikes," or, in a recent case, "response to naked aggression." The doublespeak word "terrorism" is used carefully and selectively in our press. To refer to the American bombing of Libya or the Israeli bombing of Tunis as "terrorism" would be unthinkable.

Demonstration of Doublespeak.

Arab terrorism is justifiably deplored in our press, so I will speak about another kind of terrorism, while Guillermo and I terrorize you.

[*Lights change to red.* VERDECCHIA *uses books, a stick and a flashlight to intimidate the audience, while* BROOKS *speaks through a megaphone*]

Let's talk about terrorism. Abu Nidal, Mommar Khadafy, the Red Brigade—these are baby terrorists. The real terrorists are the American government and its fascist client states. In the case of the Israeli-Palestinian conflict, it is often difficult to distinguish between acts of terrorism and acts of retaliation, and when you do, you're usually making a political judgement, not expressing fact.

The fact is, for every Israeli civilian killed by Palestinians, a lot more Palestinian and Lebanese civilians are killed by Israelis. If you need corroboration, you can look it up.

It has been the policy of certain Israeli military personnel and politicians to attack Arab civilians in order to drive them from their land, to intimidate them into accepting their fate as a conquered people, to *terrorize* them. Evidence of this policy can be found in published Israeli cabinet documents, and in the words and letters of Menachem Begin, Ariel Sharon, Yitzhak Shamir, and even...Golda Meir. If you want to know more about it, look it up. And while you are at it...

44

Look up the 1947 Der Yassin massacre led by
Menachem Begin, in which 250 defenceless Arabs were
slaughtered; look up the 1953 massacre at Quibya, in which
Ariel Sharon and his troops murdered the sleeping inhabit-
ants of an Arab village; look up the 1956 massacres in the
Gaza Strip. Look up the December 1975 bombing of a
Palestinian refugee camp that killed fifty-seven, mostly
women and children; look up the use of torture against
Arab prisoners; look up the number of Palestinians killed in
the current uprising; look up the amount of money given
to Israel by our government, by the American government,
by private citizens from both countries; look it up and then
we'll talk about terrorism.[20]

[Megaphone beep signals end of "terrorism." Lights are restored]

VERDECCHIA Thank you for your co-operation.
BROOKS Ladies and gentlemen, armed conflict and war bring
    terror and death. They bring terror and death to the occu-
    pier and occupied, to Arab and Jew, to soldier and civilian
    alike.
        Ten: Weight. Example.
        In the March 4, 1991 *Globe and Mail*, correspondent
    David Roberts wrote an in-depth article on the suffering of
    Palestinians in the West Bank during the Gulf War. He
    writes of the twenty-four-hour curfew imposed by Israel on
    Palestinians for much of the war and the resulting hard-
    ship. He writes that forty-five hundred Palestinians were
    arrested for breaking curfew. After quick military trials,
    they were fined heavily or sentenced to jail terms of up to
    five years. Roberts adds that Israel has used the war as an
    excuse to round up moderate Arabs. With such voices
    muffled, and a refusal to negotiate with the PLO, Israel will
    claim—as it has in the past—that there is no one to negoti-
    ate with.

Roberts also points out a fact known to Arab and Israeli alike: virtually all Palestinians recognize the PLO under Yasser Arafat as their only political representative body, even after the political blunder of supporting Saddam Hussein. A conquered people supporting a conqueror who claims he wants to liberate them; it may not be just, but it certainly is not surprising.

This information is available in our press. It is simply given a fraction of the weight of other stories, such as Iraqi atrocities in Kuwait, or the oil slick in the Persian Gulf.

SLIDE Oil–soaked bird from *Life* magazine

By the way, many experts believe that as much as 50 percent of the spill was caused by coalition bombs. Nevertheless, images of oil-soaked birds have set the agenda and guided our emotions into condoning this genocide. And yet we still ask a generation of Germans, "How could you let it happen?"

Demonstration of Weight.

I will now read from Roberts' article while Guillermo reviews the events of the past seven months.

[VERDECCHIA *stands on the desk with a stack of newspapers;* BROOKS *sits, reading quietly*]

VERDECCHIA Okay. August 3, 1990. The day after the Iraqi invasion of Kuwait. *The New York Post* has a picture of Saddam Hussein. "The Bully of Baghdad." Check out that moustache. Does he remind you of anybody? Yeah, me too. August 8, *The Globe and Mail*. US troops heading for Saudi Arabia. And right underneath, an article that says, "gasoline prices hit seventy cents a litre." Honk your horns if you support the Gulf War; if you didn't, don't bother, you probably don't own a car. August 10. Chemicals make front

46

page of *The Globe and Mail.* "Chemical threat sends shiver through Gulf." And on the other side of the front page, there's an article about another substance abuser, Ben Johnson. August 22. (That's my dad's birthday.) Here's a picture of a very cool, very pointy airplane doing some surgical strikes in the desert. August 28. An insect invasion stops a ball game at the Skydome. Makes the front page of *The Globe and Mail.* I don't know if you can see this photograph, but there are some very pointy insects, making some surgical strikes against this very helpless Latino ball player.

December 30. "Iraq bolsters second front at Turkish border." These cats mean business. Things are heating up, ladies and gentlemen. What else is on the front page? "Israeli army fires at Arabs, five killed, over a hundred wounded." And the Leafs lose again.

January 14. One day before the UN deadline for the withdrawal of troops from Kuwait. I have a review of *Red Tape,* a show Daniel did with the Augusta Company. I saw the show, I liked it, I didn't understand it, but this review explains it all very well, if you care to read it, here it is. One day after the deadline, guess who "lets deadline run out." This is it folks, real serious now, things are going snakey, and sure enough, January 17, the moment we've all been waiting for. "It's war!" Hit it.

[*Trini Lopez' version of "This Land Is Our Land" abruptly begins playing, then quickly fades*]

Okay. We have a very cool high-tech illustration right here, some very pointy planes going this way, some missiles that way, lots of activity on the front page. "Bombs drop as I write." "Allied planes bomb Iraq." January 18, the next day, the diagram is in colour. Iraqi missile strikes Israel. Here's the diagram which shows the Iraqi missile, very large, very pointy, going this way, the arrow indicating where it came from. According to this diagram, the Iraqi missile is about seventeen times larger than the country of Israel.

Life magazine had some fabulous photographs of the conflict, and I'd like to share some of them with you now.

SLIDE Photograph of soldier's face from the front cover of *Life*

That's an American soldier, he's got camouflage paint on, he's got a Desert Storm helmet on, he's one cool cat.

SLIDE Photograph of Marlboro cowboy

This is the back cover of *Life*, and what do you know, it's the same guy relaxing on his ranch in Montana.

SLIDE Missile launched from destroyer

Very cool, very pointy destroyer firing a missile.

SLIDE Crowd of Arabs

These are some helpless people that we are helping.

SLIDE Video image of POW

Oh, that's the POW they beat up, very weird picture from a video, very blue, very disturbing, and very very cool.

SLIDE Corpse of Kurdish woman with child

This is [*sees slide*]—oh shit.

SLIDE Soldier hugging girl

And this is an American soldier hugging a little girl.

I think *The Toronto Star* did a fabulous job covering this war. Let me show you what I mean. This is a full-page, five-colour explanation of the war. Allied assets here, Iraqi assets here. The defence, the assault. And this diagram shows it all: here's a helicopter, this is an armoured personnel carrier, this is an airplane, here's some soldiers running around, here's a little tank, bombs going off, little fires, and here's a note that says, "Note: drawing is not to scale" …and that's a good thing.

February 16. White House insists tactics are good. And who's arguing? Marlin Fitzwater said it: Iraqis have no respect for human life. What were those people doing in a bomb shelter anyway?[21]

February 22. Iraq, Soviets agree on Gulf peace plan *but* wary White House has serious concerns. And frankly, so do I. Look at this photograph. This cat has very dark, very pointy, and totally uncool sunglasses on.

February 26. US demands Saddam personally accept defeat. [*yelling*] That's right, Jack, you phone us up, we do not negotiate with radios, say *uncle!* And here's a photograph of a very cool cat with a big gun coming up over a hill, doing *The Sands of Iwo Jima* meets *Rambo.*

And of course, February 28. Cease-fire. Kuwait is liberated. Thank God this war was so short. There he is, Stormin' Norman Schwarzkopf himself. He did a great job on this war, and I'd like to thank him personally.

Now this is the March 15 "What's On" from *The Toronto Star.* Daniel and I made the front cover. I think it's safe to say that our fifteen minutes are up.

And here's today's paper. Quite an extraordinary article here on the front page, almost unbelievable. Apparently Bill Van der Zalm has been lying to the people of British Columbia. I wonder who leaked that one to the press.

But there isn't much else here. It's not half as interesting as the war, thank God it's over, but really—

Isn't peace boring? [*he jumps off the desk and returns to his seat*]

BROOKS Our final example will go without a demonstration. Some of you may have already noted that most of our major newspapers have a "Business" section, yet very few, if any, have a "Labour" section. And so ends our section on the manufacture of consent.

[BROOKS *rings a bell*]

Response to Critics

VERDECCHIA We would like to take this opportunity to respond to some of our critics. We have some. There are people who suggest that *The Noam Chomsky Lectures* is simply sour grapes. That we take shots at critics, for example, because they haven't been good to us. That is simply untrue. Here, for example, is one of several good reviews I've received from Ray Conlogue of *The Globe and Mail*:

SLIDE And Guillermo Verdecchia has some amusing moments as Galileo.[22]

And here is the one good review that Daniel has received from Geoff Chapman of *The Toronto Star:*

SLIDE Daniel Brooks manages some great twitchy moments...[23]

[BROOKS *twitches*]

So quite clearly, no sour grapes here.

We have also been told that we condemn Western, especially American, atrocities, but ignore Soviet crimes. We have been criticized for being one-sided. We have a two-tiered response to that: it is easy to condemn the Soviets and important to do so. But it is more important to protest that which we can affect. Chomsky offers the example of Soviet dissident Andrei Sakharov, who does not concern himself with Western crimes, nor do we expect him to.

Let us make ourselves perfectly clear: we do not condone Soviet aggression in the Baltics or anywhere else, we do not support terrorism of any kind, we are not Khmer Rouge apologists, nor do we deny the Holocaust. I hope that is clear.

The Auction

VERDECCHIA Nevertheless, we do wish to get a meaningful exchange happening. Therefore, part two of our response. In the spirit of the free market of ideas, we will now auction off one minute of time for a statement of any kind. May we have the house lights up, please? [*he stands*]

We'll start the bidding at one dollar and any opinion can be expressed. Swearing is optional. The bidding will begin at one dollar. Before we start, I should warn you not to scratch or make any chaotic gestures, as they might be interpreted as a bid. The bidding is open at two dollars. Two dollars for one minute of time. Have the stage and say whatever you like. Do I hear three dollars?

[BROOKS *and* VERDECCHIA *monopolize the bidding, which rapidly finishes with* BROOKS *winning at two or three thousand dollars*]

Sold to the man in the black shirt.

BROOKS I'll pay you later, Guillermo.

[**BROOKS** *stands,* **VERDECCHIA** *sits*]

First, I'd like to state that freedom of the press exists for those who own one, and we own this show.

Now Guillermo, earlier you showed us a flow chart that revealed shared interests and linkages between major corporations and media complexes. I would like to respond to that with a flow chart of my own. It's a home-made flow chart, I made it at home.

SLIDE Home made flow chart

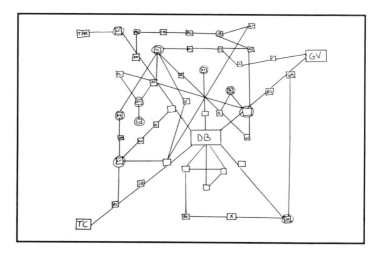

This is a sexual flow chart of my friends in the Toronto theatre community. I have put myself at the centre of the chart, simply as a matter of convenience. The boxes on the chart represent people, and the lines connecting the boxes represent sexual linkages or corporal mergers between the people. Within each box are the initials of the person represented by the box. You will note that some of the boxes are circled. The circles represent artistic directors of theatres both past and present. I would like to ask those artistic directors present tonight who do not appear on the chart to forgive me for the omission, there is no mal-intent, I simply did not want to speculate. Everything you see on the chart is based on very reliable information, and the most reliable sources are these boxes directly connected to me. You will note that I have left the initials out of these particular boxes, that's because I am not one to kiss and tell.

Let's take a closer look at the chart, shall we?

We will begin by locating Guillermo Verdecchia on the chart. There's Guillermo [*indicates with pointer*] there. Now let's trace the most direct route from me to Guillermo. I slept with this person, this person slept with that person, that person slept with this person, and this person slept with Guillermo. As you can see, he is one, two, three, four, barely a germ away. I think this gives us a hint of a rather strong inter-linkage between Guillermo and myself, a kind of shared corporal interest.

There is another route to Guillermo—I slept with her, she slept with this artistic director, he slept with her, and she also slept with the handsome, very talented, and charming Guillermo Verdecchia. There are also links between Guillermo and myself of eight, ten, twelve, and thirteen— we won't talk about thirteen, I was drunk that night.

You know, it is very interesting for me when we do the show, because each night I like to look out into the audience, see someone who is on the sexual flow chart, locate that person on the chart, and trace the most direct route to that person. It can also be very entertaining to trace a round-about route, for that can bring back many fond memories. [*he pauses, lost in brief memory*] For example, Don McKellar, one of my partners at the Augusta Company. Let's find Don on the chart. [*referring to the chart*] There I am, and one, two, three, four...there's Don. And where is the third member of the Augusta Company? [*indicates on chart*] Lying right underneath him, as it were.

Also on the chart we have "T.C.," which is one, two, three, four nights of passion away. "T.C." stands for theatre critic, a local Toronto theatre critic who we do mention in the show. We won't mention his name right now.

Up here we have "TPM" which stands for Theatre Passe Muraille. If we were to have a special flow chart of the sexual activities of our friends at Theatre Passe Muraille over the past ten, fifteen years, it would look something like this...

SLIDE Theatre Passe Muraille flow chart

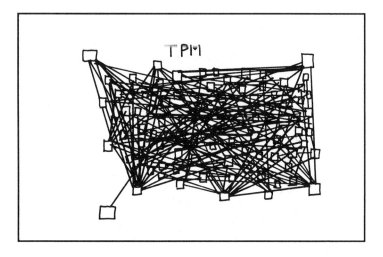

By the way, some of you may know that Theatre Passe Muraille is undergoing great financial difficulty at the present time. In fact, their general manager has told me that they are in the avant-garde of financial crisis management. We don't have time to go into why they are having such financial difficulties...let's return to the chart.

I would like to draw your attention to one linkage that comes from this dense, seething, pulsating primordial urge, and it goes directly to former Prime Minister Pierre Eliot Trudeau.

Finally, I would like to say that the reason I am showing these charts, Guillermo, is not to give the people the impression that all we do in the theatre is fuck. We do fuck a lot, there is no question about that, but we do other things. We work in restaurants, ride our bikes, dine with our families, and sometimes we even make theatre. No. The reason I have publicly displayed these charts is to show the people that we are part of a community, and that within any community there are shared interests, shared ideas, shared ideologies, shared lives. For instance, I don't think anyone represented on this chart supports Free Trade, but I do think it's safe to say that everyone on this chart and everyone on the previous chart is a strong advocate of government support for the arts.[24]

Audience Opinion Poll

VERDECCHIA Thank you, Daniel. We will now conduct an audience opinion poll. Lights up on the house please.

BROOKS Those of you who were in support of the American invasion of Panama, or as *The Toronto Star* termed it, "The American attack on Noriega," please raise a hand...

SLIDE Front page of *The Toronto Star*, with headline "US ATTACKS NORIEGA"

Those of you who approved of the invasion please raise a hand...[25]

SLIDE Canada does not approve of third party intervention anywhere in Central America.
— Prime Minister Brian Mulroney, September 15, 1986

Doesn't matter, the question was rhetorical. House lights off, please.
One of the first acts by the Canadian government as a

member of the Organization of American States, was indeed to approve of the invasion of Panama…

SLIDE We believe the United States acted correctly in these particular circumstances.
— Prime Minister Brian Mulroney, December, 1989

…even though it very clearly violated the charter upon which the Organization of American States was founded.

SLIDE The territory of a state is inviolable; it may not be the object of a military occupation on any ground whatsoever.
— ARTICLE 20, Charter of the Organization of American States

Now, be it that we live in a democratic society, and in a democratic society the government expresses the will of the people, the government *is* the people, we all approved of the invasion of Panama.

In fact, the voting line of the Canadian government in institutions such as the United Nations, the International Monetary Fund, and the World Bank, consistently follows the American line, attesting to our hypocrisy vis à vis our alleged concern for human rights, and what the hell is this war on drugs scam, for God's sake, it was Bush who got Noriega started in the drug business in the first place, and all this bullshit really ties my nuts up in a tight knot and…

[VERDECCHIA *blows the Whistle of Indignation*]

VERDECCHIA The Whistle of Indignation has been blown. Daniel is experiencing the same emotion that his character is going through at the present time; he is in the throes of an…

56

SLIDE Honest Emotion

...honest emotion. I will now...

SLIDE noitacinummoC

...etacinummoc some ideas to you in the hope of...

SLIDE Engagement

...engaging you, and show my commitment to the characters onstage...

SLIDE Commitment to the characters on the stage

...Daniel's character in particular—Daniel has been left stranded on stage with nothing to do—by giving Daniel something to do. Daniel, please fall down.

[BROOKS *falls*]

Silence and Falling

VERDECCHIA Daniel will fall down a number of times. Each fall represents 100 civilians killed by government forces in El Salvador last year. Anytime, Daniel.

[BROOKS *falls twelve times during the following speech;* VERDECCHIA *keeps count, putting up a finger for each fall*]

El Salvador's recent elections passed almost unnoticed in our press. The elections took place in a climate of terror and intimidation. The bombing of residential neighbourhoods by El Salvadorean armed forces, the death squad

murders of sleeping civilians, the detention and torture of
El Salvadorean journalists, the gasoline fire which destroyed
the lone opposition newspaper, the murder of an opposition politician, and the death threats made against several
others received only minimal attention. A Reuter's dispatch
to the March 11, 1991 *Toronto Star* contextualized the
electoral violence by explaining that the March 10 elections
were the first elections in eleven years that had not been
disrupted by the guerrilla forces of the FMLN. The above-
mentioned government-sponsored disruptions were not
mentioned in the article.

In contrast, the execution of British journalist Farzad
Bazoft and the death threat against British citizen Salman
Rushdie received an extraordinary amount of attention.
Mr. Rushdie was featured in 184 articles in *The Globe* in
1989. It would not be unfair to conclude that there is a
racist bias in our press where some victims are more worthy
than others.[26]

Digression

VERDECCHIA At this point, I'd like to digress and come downstage to read you a letter I sent to Geoff Chapman.

[VERDECCHIA *sits at the edge of the stage alongside* BROOKS, *who
has remained lying down since the final fall*]

"Dear Mr. Chapman: In your article surveying the
Governor-General's Awards"—Mr. Chapman calls them
the "Gee Gees"—"you state that the themes of
homophobia, racism, and the problems of coming out,
explored in the play *Black Friday?* are familiar ones, that
we've heard enough about them. You go so far as to suggest
that these problems have been conquered in Toronto.

58

In the parts of Toronto that I frequent, homosexuals, people of colour, and women still face daily harassment, discrimination, and the threat of physical violence.

"Included in your dismissal of [the play] *Scientific Americans* is a summary dismissal of what you call the military-industrial bogeyman. You are of course entitled to your opinions, but are you aware that as much as 50 per-cent of the Canadian weapons industry is foreign-owned and controlled? Such a structure has far-reaching moral and economic consequences for many people. Surely you recognize that the military-industrial complex is a structure built on inefficiency and waste.

"In short Mr. Chapman, I am profoundly disturbed by the way in which you, someone who has the opportunity to speak to several thousand people daily, dismiss problems which have enormous consequences for all of us, because they interfere with your enjoyment of 'zippy' pacing and plays 'with and on words.' Sincerely, Guillermo Verdecchia."

[VERDECCHIA *stands up, and* BROOKS *returns to the desk*]

SLIDE The highest value proclaimed in the intellectual culture must be total ignorance about who we are and what we do in the world.
— Noam Chomsky, *The Culture of Terrorism*

Some of you may be thinking that what we have em-barked on here is not theatre. Well, that's too bad. I would like to say this: if the theatre is to survive, it must become something other than an expensive alternative to television. We are going to have to look at the world and the world of the theatre without ideological or artistic blinders. And I'm not talking about the theatre of gentle psychological manipulation, or mature content, or three-dimensional characters. I'm talking about rolling up our sleeves, diving into the muck, taking a good, hard look at who we are and what we do and goddamn the excuses.

[**BROOKS** *smashes the Artstick.* **VERDECCHIA** *returns to the desk*][27]

Marketing Plan

SLIDE Footnotes, selected bibliography, and T-shirts are available.

VERDECCHIA Daniel, we've been talking about moving *The Noam Chomsky Lectures* to a larger space. I was wondering if you had any ideas for a marketing plan.

BROOKS Why yes, I have some ideas in front of me, Guillermo. Now, if we are going to move to a larger theatre, we are going to need more people in the theatre. After all, what is theatre but a bunch of people in a room together, some who pay, some who get payed.... We need more payers, Guillermo. Now, Guillermo Verdecchia and Daniel Brooks are not exactly household names. In order to increase the profile of the show, we should get some names on stage. Here are a few I'm considering: Gordon Pinsent; Barbara Frum; Al Waxman as Manuel Noriega; perhaps Mr. T as Brian Mulroney and Frank Sinatra as Saddam Hussein...both non-traditional casting, both have a kind of symmetry; and finally, Wayne Gretzky as Noam Chomsky.

VERDECCHIA The Great One.

BROOKS Gretzky might be a little expensive, he makes about as much per year as twenty thousand Bolivians. If we can't afford Gretzky, perhaps we could get a lot of Bolivian extras.

In order to get more payers, I feel we need more sexual content in the show.

[VERDECCHIA *begins taking off his shirt*]

That is why Guillermo is taking off his shirt. But, once he gets his shirt off you will see that there's not quite enough sexual content there. Guillermo, by the way, is the Spanish for William, or Willy, but he won't be showing us that. So, in order to up the sexual content of the show, we are currently negotiating with Crow's Theatre, and we hope to borrow one or two breasts from any one of their past productions.

And finally, Guillermo, the poster. We do have a poster, but it's a little arty, and well, quite frankly, a little *little*. We need a bigger poster. I made a mock-up of it and brought it down to the theatre in order to show the people, but I couldn't get it through the double doors. This is the mother of all posters.

I feel that the poster should have the following boldly printed on it: "Four shows only. Limited seating. Show must close. Will sell out." Then, when it comes time for people to call in and reserve tickets—the phone number should be something easy to remember…ah…Chomsky has seven letters, just dial *C-H-O-M-S-K-Y*—when the people call in, we'll take the phone off the hook. They will get a busy signal and think, My God, it's busy, it's constantly busy, we'll never get tickets, it's a hit…. They will call and call again, they will panic and talk to their friends, the word will spread, and finally, after two days, we'll put the phone back on the hook, take reservations, and extend the run to the previously planned five weeks.

VERDECCHIA Good plan, Daniel. Thank you.[28]

Public Service Announcement

VERDECCHIA We have some do's and don't's.

61

Do write letters to editors.

Do attend rallies and teach-ins to make connections between local, domestic and foreign policy issues.

Do boycott El Salvadorean coffee.

Do stoop and scoop when your pets poop prolifically.

Do disobey, disrupt, and dissent.

BROOKS Don't put yourself in a position where you profit by another's misery.

Don't drive an eight-cylinder automobile across town to pick up a used copy of Ayn Rand's *The Fountainhead.*

Don't wipe your boogers on other people's furniture, it's not fair.

Don't be fooled by the "new" in new world order.
And...

Don't forget that the Israeli military and economy depend on the over three billion dollars in aid provided annually by the United States, and as the United States forges stronger military ties with other Arab nations, they will need Israel less, so...

Don't forget that security for the state of Israel depends on making peace with her neighbours, so I appeal to my fellow Jews to demand that Israel negotiate with the PLO and consider giving up the Occupied Territories. And, please...

Don't call critics of Israeli foreign policy anti-Semites, it's stupid, and...

Don't forget I've been to Israel, I have friends there, one friend who would appear on a sexual flow chart in a different country, so...

Don't call me a self-hating Jew. I hate that, I really hate that. It pulls on my circumcised penis and sends my kreplach right up into my eyeballs...

[*Whistle of Indignation is blown*]

Dramaturgy

VERDECCHIA Daniel and I recognize that this show lacks…
narrative. Narrative is traditionally considered to be a very
important element of any theatrical presentation. We have
a narrative we would like to share with you. A little mood
lighting please.

[*Lights dim.* BROOKS *and* VERDECCHIA *inch their chairs closer to
the audience*]

SLIDE Photograph of a river valley

BROOKS The hero of our tale is a gentleman named Miguel.
He is a tireless worker for human rights and human dig-
nity in countries such as El Salvador, Guatemala, and
Nicaragua. In our story, Miguel has worked hard for the
revolution in Nicaragua and has seen many dreams real-
ized. In that country, literacy rates have shot up, infant
mortality rates have dropped, land has been distributed to
formerly landless and hopeless peasants, schools and hospitals have been built. But alas, the American economic war
against the country has made a shambles of the economy,
and their proxy army, the contras, has attacked villages,
farms, and hospitals. In one such attack, Miguel's wife
and two children are killed.

His dreams are shattered, and he is despairing. He sits
by the side of the road on a hot day. He has a machete in
his right hand.

[VERDECCHIA *raises a butcher knife*]

He looks at the veins on his left wrist and realizes that
with a single blow he could end it all. He raises the machete and is about to bring it down on his life when he

hears a donkey coming down the road. On the donkey is a young boy. He has a coconut under his arm.

[VERDECCHIA *holds up an apple*]

He approaches Miguel, dismounts, and with a gallant wave of his huge sombrero greets Miguel and says, "I haven't eaten for days. May I borrow your machete to open my coconut?" Miguel gives him the machete and the hungry boy cuts open the coconut...

[VERDECCHIA *cuts the apple*]

...giving half to Miguel...

[VERDECCHIA *gives half of the apple to* BROOKS]

...and keeping half for himself. And as he is about to eat, Miguel realizes that at the age of thirty-one, he has been reborn.

[BROOKS *and* VERDECCHIA *eat*]²⁹

Last Part

SLIDE We live entangled in webs of endless deceit, in a highly indoctrinated society in which elementary truths are easily hidden.
— Noam Chomsky, *Turning The Tide*

VERDECCHIA [*reading*] "We live entangled in webs of endless deceit, often self-deceit, but with a little honest effort, it is possible to extricate ourselves from them. If we do, we will learn that our own actions, or passive acquiescence

64

contribute quite substantially to misery and oppression and perhaps eventual global destruction. But there is a brighter side. We are fortunate to live in a society that is relatively free and open. We are free to act in many ways to bring about crucial changes in policy and even more fundamental institutional changes. We are fortunate, perhaps uniquely so, in the range of opportunities we enjoy for free inquiry and effective action."[30]

We of *The Noam Chomsky Lectures* wish to thank you for hearing us out.

SLIDE The United States can at least count on our quiet acquiescence.
— Mark MacGuigan, minister of external affairs

BROOKS What we'll do now is show you one last slide. We will turn to the slide, and the lights will go to black as we exit. We ask that you consider the slide in the dark. When any one of you has had enough, you will yell, "Light!" The lights will come up, and the show will be over...

[**BROOKS** *and* **VERDECCHIA** *exit as lights fade*]

SLIDE The question for Canadians is whether they feel comfortable being accomplices to mass murder. In the past the answer has been yes, they do feel comfortable.
— Noam Chomsky, *Language and Politics*

Member of the audience calls "Light." Lights restored

The End

Notes

In order to give the reader an idea as to how *The Noam Chomsky Lectures* has developed over time, we offer some alternate readings. Each time we perform the show, we re-write certain sections in order to address current world events, changes in the local cultural scene, and the circumstances of production (the theatre in which we perform, the sponsors of the event, etc.) and, ultimately, the connections between all the above.

We would also like to remind you that the preceding script of *The Noam Chomsky Lectures* is little more than a transcript of one performance which took place on March 31, 1991 at Theatre Passe Muraille in Toronto—the tail end of a run of shows that began on March 12, 1991. This show was a substantially reworked version of previous shows, and was revised so that we could address the most recent tragedy on the international stage—the Gulf War.

The authors recognize that the play's grammar falters at times, that we slip into vernacular usages. Chomsky writes that distinctions between "high" and "low" uses of language are expressions of political hierarchy, not of relative merit. We have chosen to let "mistakes" stand as is (or as are?).

Finally, we ask that you excuse the informality of the bibliography and notes. This is not an academic paper, but the transcript of a performance of what we like to think is a popular-theatre genre. If you would like to know the source of a particular fact or statement and its source is not cited, please feel free to contact us, D.B. and G.V., in care of the publisher.

1 Toronto's Dora Mavor Moore Awards recognize excellence in the art of theatre.

2 The Wooster Group was perhaps the first theatre company to do "table plays." As much as we appreciate the work of the Wooster Group, we reject comparisons of *The Noam Chomsky Lectures* to the Wooster Group's work as superficial. The comparisons were so numerous that we felt it necessary to incorporate a disclaimer.

3 From *Globe and Mail* theatre critic Ray Conlogue's review of Nightwood Theatre's *Princess Pocahantas*, February 12, 1990.

4 From Ray Conlogue's reviews of Quebec dance troupe La La La Human Steps, and the play *Princess Pocahantas*, respectively.

5 From Ray Conlogue's review of Robert Lepage and Gordon McCall's production of *Romeo and Juliette*.

6 One could easily write a book in order to reveal linkages between board members of these corporations and the American government, the American military, and American intelligence services, including the CIA.

7 When *The Noam Chomsky Lectures* was first produced, Robert Crew was the theatre critic for *The Toronto Star*, the largest circulation newspaper in Canada. Hence, this section was addressed to him:

BROOKS *White Trash/Blue Eyes* is a show recently presented here in Toronto. It is a transparent, I repeat, transparent condemnation of corporate greed and a plea for community values. Here are two samples of the text: "The truly needy people get what they need. Those who don't, don't need as much." And this next one was sung by the chairman of the board as a kind of pep talk for his charges: "The word is in WIN, WIN with a 'W,' the 'I' is the word that you heard from me and it's the letter in the center of WIN." "I" and "WIN." Wrote Robert Crew of the show, "I didn't ever get to grips with the central themes being presented."

Well ladies and gentlemen, grip this...

It should be noted that the most consistent criticism we receive when the show is performed in Toronto is that we are not harsh enough with Ray Conlogue, whose critical writings are viewed by many as misogynistic, racist, and insidiously dull-witted. Many believe that because the ideological assumptions in his writing are less visible, Mr. Conlogue's critical opus is far more damaging than that of either Crew or Chapman.

8 From Wallace Clement's *The Canadian Corporate Elite* (Carleton University Press, 1986).

9 The section of the play following "Any questions?" is designed to allow the authors to discuss current events, as well as issues that relate closely to the venue in which the show is taking place. This section was first created for a performance at the DuMaurier World Stage Festival in Toronto. The festival was heavily subsidized by the tobacco company, and the stage was festooned with DuMaurier flags that looked like glorious cigarette packages:

BROOKS Yes, Guillermo, I have a question. It states in the contract that we signed with Harbourfront in order to bring this humble little show to these good people—it states, and I quote: "The company"—that's us Guillermo—"the company shall not take any action which would derogate in any manner from the rights or privileges of any sponsor of Harbourfront either in connection with the Attraction or otherwise."

Now, does that mean we are not allowed to derogate DuMaurier, the main sponsors of this festival, but that we are allowed to derogate the company that owns them, Imperial Tobacco? Or, are we perhaps not allowed to derogate Imperial Tobacco, but are allowed to derogate the company that owns them, IMASCO? Or are we not allowed to derogate IMASCO, but are allowed to derogate one of their subsidiaries, for instance, Shopper's Drug Mart, United Cigar Stores, or Genstar Properties Limited? If not, then are we allowed to derogate the company that owns IMASCO, the enormous British Conglomorate B.A.T., which also owns the American Batus Inc., which owns Kent, Kool, Lucky Strike, Viceroy, Saks Fifth Avenue, lots of land, and maybe the building you live in? Or, if we were to derogate any other corporation that the board members of B.A.T. control, would it be a breach of contract and so threaten the $150 that each of us was paid?

The second time the "Any questions?" section was performed was at the Fringe Festival of Toronto. Guy Sprung had recently been fired as artistic director of Canadian Stage Company.

BROOKS Yes, Guillermo, I have a question. Here we are at the Fringe Festival, with over fifty companies, countless actors, writers, directors, designers. In the meantime, there has been a great kaffufle over at Canadian Stage, Toronto's largest not-for-profit theatre company.

The question is, Guillermo, should we be concerned? Should we be concerned that a corporate board has fired Canadian Stage's artistic director Guy Sprung?

Or, should we be concerned that people who had consistently criticized and insulted Mr. Sprung are now springing to his defence?

Or, should we be concerned that before the firing of the bearded Sprung there was little response to the absurd deficit of Canadian Stage or to their consistent inability to effectively develop a Canadian playwriting programme?

Or, should we be concerned that there was no organized resistance when Toronto Free Theatre and Centre Stage merged to form Canadian Stage in the first place, even though the two theatres had nothing in common other than having artistic directors with beards? Should we be concerned?

When performed at Glendon College in Toronto some six months later, after Canadian Stage had changed the programming for the upcoming season from a gush of original Canadian works to a trickle, the following was added:

BROOKS Their corporate board recently fired the artistic director, secured a $500,000 loan from Metro Council, and this, the third-largest theatre in the country, opened their 1990-91 season with a show by David Mamet, an American, and a show by Oscar Wilde, a dead Irishman.

10 The transcript of this meeting appeared in the October 1990 issue of *Harper's* magazine. It was arranged by the Iraqi embassy in Washington. Before the Gulf War brought Saddam Hussein to *The Noam Chomsky Lectures*, we used a fundraising letter written by Rear Admiral John Poindexter, as reprinted in the February 1990 issue of *Harper's*. Poindexter was Reagan's national security adviser from 1985 to 1986. In June 1990, he was sentenced to six months in prison for lying to Congress about his involvement in the Iran-contra scandal. For the reading of Poindexter's letter, both BROOKS and VERDECCHIA wore oversized Uncle Sam hats and spoke in grotesque American accents. The letter, in an edited version, read:

BROOKS "Dear Fellow American, because I care more about the long-term security of America than I do about myself, I must now face the liberals' accusations surrounding the 'Iran-contra affair.' And as I stand, one man, alone against the massive onslaught of liberal special interests who want to imprison me for serving my country, I must now turn to you for help.

VERDECCHIA "I'm only one man, standing up to fight for what the American flag really means to people struggling to be free.

BROOKS "I'm only one man, and the liberals want me silenced. The liberals want me bankrupt or imprisoned.

VERDECCHIA "That's why I had to write to you today. As a former US Navy admiral, I'm used to giving orders, not asking for help. But today, I ask you to make your most generous contribution to the Poindexter Defense Fund. Thank you in advance for your support and God bless you.

BROOKS "Sincerely, John M. Poindexter, Rear Admiral, US Navy, Retired." Guillermo and I will be taking donations on behalf of Admiral Poindexter. Please put them in the hats Guillermo is presently placing at the front of the stage.

11 One hundred thousand Iraqi dead is a conservative figure that does not include the many thousands more who have died and are still dying from disease and starvation. The country's infrastructure has been decimated.

12 As stated in her review of *The Noam Chomsky Lectures*.

13 According to John Judge, in a lecture he delivered at the University of Toronto on August 9, 1991, one of the best-kept secrets of the post-war years is the enormous number of American war vets who have committed suicide (between three and four times the number of Americans killed in action). In other words, a substantial number of Americans managed to "kick the Vietnam syndrome" long before Bush managed to do so with the Gulf War.

14 Much of our information on Vietnam comes from Victor Levant's book, *Quiet Complicity* (Between the Lines, 1986).

15 The ironic use of the phrase "returning to reality" is Chomsky's own.

16 The two primary sources for this section are *Human Rights in Canadian Foreign Policy*, edited by Robert O. Matthews and Cranford Pratt (McGill-Queen's University Press, 1985) and *Human Rights, Development, and Foreign Policy: Canadian Perspectives*, edited by Irving Brecher (Institute for Research on Public Policy, 1989).

The "Lecture" section is rewritten for each new production of the play. We include here three different versions of the "Lecture." The first was written for performance in May, 1990, shortly before presidential elections were to be held in Nicaragua:

VERDECCHIA Noam Chomsky's thoroughly-documented writings consistently demolish the necessary illusion that a concern for democracy motivates the actions of the United States in Panama or Vietnam. He also shatters the myth that the press is left-leaning, independent, and critical of government activity. Chomsky demonstrates very clearly how the media contains debate within very narrow boundaries. Although our Canadian press has a measure of independence from the American press, we still rely heavily on American sources. Check your *Toronto Star* or your *Globe and Mail* and see how often they quote a White House official or an American expert. We will present here briefly, and by no means exhaustively, a model for what Professor Chomsky refers to as the political economy of human rights and the political economy of the mass media. Our discussion will focus on Nicaragua.

Since 1981, the American government has pursued a policy of destabilization. After the revolution that over-threw Somoza, the US cut off all aid to Nicaragua and refused a request for training and arms, claiming that Cuban arms had passed through Nicaragua en route to the guerrillas in El Salvador. They then mobilized the proxy army which we know and love as the contras, or, as Uncle Ronald called them, "freedom fighters."

The American argument, supported by the American press and sometimes challenged by *Globe and Mail* editori-als, is that the contras are a necessary force required to put Nicaragua back into the Central American mode. Are the contras democracy-loving Nicaraguan patriots fighting for a more egalitarian—a kinder, gentler—Nicaragua?

Let's examine the facts.

The contras are led by friends to former dictator Anastasio Somoza, a man once referred to by an American president as, "a son of a bitch, but he's our son of a bitch." The contra leaders are land-owners and managers for Coca-Cola, known as one of the most repressive enterprises in Central America. The contra leaders receive an annual salary of eighty-four thousand dollars from the CIA. Among them is Arturo Cruz, the great Nicaraguan patriot who has lived in Nicaragua for a grand total of one year from 1960 to 1985.

SLIDE The purpose of aid is to permit people who are fighting on our side to use more violence.
— Eliot Abrams, assistant secretary of state

The contras have failed to establish any kind of popular base for their activities. Lacking support, the contras have avoided any kind of confrontation with the Nicaraguan military and have concentrated on "soft targets." Soft targets include schools, medical centres, and co-operative farms. Apparently, the continued contra presence was too much for Nicaraguan President Daniel Ortega. So in October of last year he called off a cease-fire—a decision that much outraged Uncle George. *The Toronto Star*, home to Bob [Crew], Henry [Mietkiewicz], and Vit [Wagner, the newspaper's three drama critics,] ran a front-page article on the end of the cease-fire which devoted seven paragraphs to Uncle George and the White House, two paragraphs to contra leader Adolfo Calero, and one to President Ortega's actual statements. No mention was made of the fact that the cease-fire had been unilateral, that is, declared by the Nicaraguan government alone. In other words, the contras were free to run around the Nicaraguan countryside spending their so-called "humanitarian aid" destroying farms while the Nicaraguan army stayed put in the naïve hope that if you ignore nasty contras maybe they will go away. The contras were supposed to disband on December 8, 1989 but they've decided to stick around for a while longer. The fact that the contras and their Washington masters ignored the December 8 deadline was entirely overlooked in our press, except for one reference, January 12 in *The Globe and Mail*, also known as the boss's paper or The Paper You Can't Get Delivered to Your House if You Live in the Wrong Part of Town. (Advertisers want to know that they are reaching a high-income readership. Hence, *The Globe and Mail* no longer delivers to certain low-income neighbourhoods in Toronto.)

In 1984 the contras mined Nicaragua's harbours. Nicaragua took its case to the World Court and the Court condemned the action as it clearly violated International Law. The American press responded by referring to the World Court as a "hostile forum." At the same time, Congress voted on more contra aid because contras were "the only way to get the Sandinistas to negotiate seriously." This statement was made five days after Nicaragua had accepted the latest draft of the Contadora Peace Act.

SLIDE Nicaragua may be beyond the reach of our good intentions.
— Jefferson Morley, *The New York Times*

The Sandinistas agreed to the Contadora Act in 1984, the first country to do so. The US then demanded changes to that draft. The Sandinistas have, in fact, bent over backwards to try and reach some kind of agreement. They have agreed to Contadora, complied with the Arias plan, and repeatedly called for international monitoring of their borders. For a full discussion of the "peace process," I refer you to Noam Chomsky's *The Culture of Terrorism*.

The press refuses to recognize the fact that Nicaragua's first free elections were held in 1984. Press coverage at the time was sketchy. We did not hear, for example, from the Latin American Studies Association who monitored the elections and found them to be "by Latin American standards a model of probity and fairness."

For an in-depth comparison of the Salvadorean and Nicaraguan elections, I refer you to Noam Chomsky and Edward S. Herman's *Manufacturing Consent*.

We didn't hear much about the election itself, but we did hear about the alleged delivery of Soviet MIG-21 fighter planes to Nicaragua. To quote Chomsky, "Although the MIGs weren't there, and the timing was perfect to divert attention from a successful election, the elite media asked no questions." The media chose to focus on what the Reagan administration might do if MIGs were delivered. This tactic allowed the whole frame of discourse to shift to the assumption that Nicaragua had indeed done something intolerable. The government was allowed to set the agenda for the debate. The Latin America Studies Association found that "the final results were not even reported in the international press. They were buried under an avalanche of alarmist news reports." The Sandinistas, by the way, won.

Chomsky and co-writer Edward Herman discuss this deliberate distortion and suppression of facts in their book, *Manufacturing Consent*.

The following was written for a June 1990 performance at the DuMaurier World Stage Festival. It was a response to the shocking defeat of the Sandinistas in the Nicaraguan elections that had taken place on February 25, 1990.

VERDECCHIA June 10—three days from now—is the deadline for contra disarmament. They have been around for ten years now. Let's look at some of the highlights of their activities.

1979: Dictator Anastasio Somoza fled to Miami while National Guard commanders were evacuated in American planes, planes disguised with Red Cross markings. This little trick was a flagrant violation of the Geneva Convention. The National Guard, incidentally, was established by the Americans in 1933. Their leader was Anastasio Somoza I. The Argentine military was used to arm and train the contras.

After intense pressure from US banks, who feared a default on Somoza's loans and huge losses, the US gave Nicaragua seventy million dollars in aid. Sixty percent of this was for the private sector, and part of it was in the form of credits to buy US goods. One of the conditions of the aid was that no money should go to projects using Cuban personnel—ensuring that, as Cubans were involved in Nicaraguan education and health care, none of the money would go to Nicaraguan schools or hospitals or collective farms.

The US refused a Sandinista request for arms and training and blocked efforts to obtain them from other Western countries. For example, the US blocked the purchase of Mirage jets from France. Not surprisingly, Nicaragua turned to Eastern bloc countries for aid and military support.

As these facts pass through the media filters, they are transformed. For example: February 27, a *Globe and Mail* article entitled "The End of the Revolution," authored by Maurice Tugwell, founder of the Mackenzie Institute for the Study of Terrorism, Revolution, and Propaganda. In his article Mr. Tugwell claims, "Washington assisted the Sandinistas until that regime bit the hand that fed it." Clearly, Washington did fuck-all for the Sandinistas.

Mr. Tugwell, considered an expert on terrorism by various Canadian media sources, and a consultant for the Canadian military, was a former intelligence officer with the British army. While working in Ireland, Mr. Tugwell manufactured a number of IRA atrocity stories. In Canada, he was a director for the pro-apartheid Canadian-South African Society. He also serves as an advisor to companies such as DOW Chemical, advising them how to deal with environmentalists—terrorists in sheep's clothing.

1981: US takes over direct funding and training for the contras.

1984: US helps the contras mine Nicaraguan harbours.

1985: Private American aid to the contras almost equals American government aid to the contras.

1987: Contra death toll reaches its peak; 5,339 are killed in that year.

In the meantime, Nicaragua has agreed to two drafts of the Contadora Peace Act. Both were scuttled by US pressure. Nicaragua began granting amnesty to contras in 1983.

Nicaragua and other Central American nations sign the Esquipulas II Accord.

1989: After a number of summits, the Central American presidents agree on a plan to demobilize the contras. They repeat their demand that all outside funding of irregular forces be halted. December 5 is set as the date for the demobilization of the contra bases in Honduras. Nothing comes of this agreement. On December 10, at the San Isidro Summit, the Central American presidents ask the US to transfer contra funds to observer groups to aid in the demobilization process. This passes without attention in our press except for one reference January 12 in *The Globe and Mail*. The Bush administration claims the contras are required in order to ensure free and fair elections in February.

The US-backed UNO coalition won the elections.

The Canadian and American press were virtually unanimous in their enthusiasm for this triumph of democracy. *The Globe*, for example, told us that "the Sandinistas went down to defeat after a decade of one-party rule." *The Star* explained that "Nicaraguans chose freely when at last given the chance to do so." The obvious was, of course, unstated. One: Nicaragua had already held free and fair elections, the first in their history, in 1984. Two: only a totalitarian of a rather special bent would refer to the recent elections as free and fair when the contra threat was ever-present. It was made clear to Nicaraguans that if the Sandinistas were re-elected, the United States would continue its devastating trade embargo and continue to fund the contras and fuel the violence that was shattering Nicaragua. The Nicaraguan people chose to vote for the party that had the connections to end the war.

April 18: The contras sign an accord with representatives of UNO stating that demobilization would begin on April 25 and end on June 10.

May 4: President Chamorro and contra leader Franklin sign a declaration stating that demobilization would begin simultaneously in five security zones.

May 8: The first contras disarm. Ninety-four of them hand over some unserviceable assault rifles.

Two weeks later, the contras break off talks with the government, claiming fourteen contras had been killed by members of a Sandinista co-operative. No evidence was found to substantiate the claim.

May 30, another accord is signed. The contras agree to disarm at the rate of five hundred per day in zones protected by other contras. There are about twelve thousand contras in Nicaragua at the time. Do your own calculations and see how many times five hundred goes into twelve thousand. The June 12 deadline seems a little optimistic. Of course, there is always the remote possibility that the contras have no intention of fully demobilizing. After all, fifteen hundred contras have returned to Honduras where they have family members. We should also bear in mind that the US has expressed some dissatisfaction with President Chamorro's decision to retain Humberto Ortega as head of the army. As the Inter-Church Committee on Human Rights in Latin America (ICCHRLA) has pointed out, "however many accords are signed...the death and destruction being inflicted on the Nicaraguan people ...cannot be halted without the acquiescence of the US."

The following was written for a performance at Glendon College in Toronto. The performance was on January 14, 1990, the eve of the United Nations deadline for the withdrawal of Iraqi troops from Kuwait, and three days before the start of the Gulf War:

VERDECCHIA On August 2, Iraqi troops invaded Kuwait, installed a puppet government, and later annexed it outright. Tomorrow marks the UN deadline for the withdrawal of Iraqi troops, after which the use of force is authorized. Canadian troops may engage in battle for the first time in forty years.

The Globe and Mail has called Saddam Hussein the "butcher of Baghdad." Maclean's has called Baghdad a "city that openly glorifies death." Frank Jones of The Toronto Star has called Hussein a "mad dog." Ray Conlogue, theatre critic for The Globe and Mail, has compared Hussein to Cyrus, King of ancient Persia. Other, less obtuse comparisons have been made with Hitler. Our very own Prime Minister Brian "let's tax books" Mulroney has called Hussein a "criminal of historic proportions."

Our press has also sought to keep ever-present in our minds the daily horror of life under the Iraqi regime. A front-page article December 15 in The Star described the torture and rape of Kuwaiti prisoners by Iraqi troops. On January 7, The Star ran another front-page article describing Iraqi destruction and explaining that British Prime Minister John Major "denounced Iraqi atrocities."

A January 3 article in *The Star* offered this perspective: "Bush said that he had further hardened against Saddam after reading a recent report by Amnesty International on Iraqi actions in Kuwait.... 'It was so terrible, it's hard to describe,' Bush said. 'I handed it to Barbara...and she read about two pages of it and said, "I can't read any more." The torturing of a handicapped child.... It's outrageous what's happened,' he said."

Clearly, Saddam Hussein is a criminal, his invasion of Kuwait is a gross violation of International Law, and his regime is undoubtedly a consistent violator of human rights. What may not be so obvious are the distortions of context or the outright lack of context in reportage, the element of caricature, and the double standards that condemn his actions while condoning similar atrocities by the United States and its allies.

After all, Hussein's excuse for the invasion of Kuwait, "the right to defend our interests," is the same excuse as that offered by the US for its invasion of Grenada and Panama and for its proxy war on Nicaragua. Our press has avoided any comparison of the Iraqi invasion of Kuwait with recent American adventures. Comparisons with the 1982 Israeli attack on Southern Lebanon, or the 1967 annexation of the Syrian Golan Heights, or the genocidal Indonesian invasion of East Timor have all been avoided.

We must also ask ourselves, when was the last time *The Toronto Star* ran a front-page article describing the torture and murder of hundreds of civilians in El Salvador and Guatemala, two countries (among many others) propped up by the United States, where torture is systematic? We might also ask whether or not George and Barbara ever read any Amnesty reports on the situation in Central America.

Incidentally, on December 1 the Guatemalan military massacred twenty-four unarmed Guatemalan peasants.

This event passed with little notice in our press.

Our press has also glossed over the fact that during the Iran-Iraq war in the eighties, the US supplied money and arms and provided military assistance to both sides in the conflict. In April 1990, the assistant secretary of state for the Middle East testified before Congress that the US had no commitment to defend Kuwait. On July 25, with Iraqi troops massed along the Kuwaiti border, the US ambassador to Kuwait met with Hussein. The ambassador told Hussein that the US had no opinion on the Iraqi-Kuwaiti border dispute. Hussein explained that Kuwait's actions—slant drilling into an Iraqi oil field and exceeding production quotas—amounted to economic war and that, if a peaceful solution could not be found, obviously Iraq could not "accept death."

The US ambassador gave no warning that the US would oppose any move by Iraq against Kuwait. Instead, she told Hussein, "I have a direct instruction from the president to seek better relations with Iraq." Two days before the invasion, the assistant secretary of state for the Middle East again testified publicly to the effect that the US had no commitment to defend Kuwait. And, according to the head of the Senate Intelligence Commitee, the CIA had predicted the invasion four days before it happened.

Our press has chosen not to ask why there was no public or private warning to Hussein, and why there was no effort to create international opposition while there was still time. It is of course possible that the US was looking for this sort of confrontation, or simply was surprised by the extent of the Iraqi invasion. This kind of speculation is, however, far from our mainstream press.

Our press instead has chosen to focus on Bush's "extra mile," the now failed peace initiative. A January 4 article in The Globe, with the headline "Bush Offers Last Chance to Iraq," explained that there would be no negotiations, no compromises, and that Bush's peace effort serves to "neutralize European and other efforts to mediate the Gulf crisis." We have also been told that Hussein's August 12 proposal to address all the outstanding conflicts of the region is unacceptable.

We are never told why the US wishes to neutralize other efforts or why the Iraqi proposal was rejected.

A *Globe* column by Jeffrey Simpson may provide a clue. Mr. Simpson writes, "Suppose Saddam Hussein does decide to withdraw from Kuwait.... Iraq's neighbours would still have reason to fear his militaristic designs and delusions of Iraqi grandeur.... [A] peaceful resolution would leave intact Iraq's military arsenal." Mr. Simpson does not choose to inform us that the purchase of Iraq's overrated military arsenal (Iraq did spend the last decade unable to defeat Iran in a war) was made possible through loans and trade credits from the West.

We should also bear in mind that the UN resolution does not authorize the elimination of Hussein, or the destruction of the Iraqi arsenal. Students of history will note the parallel with Korea.

17 During the Oka crisis in Quebec in the summer of 1990, Prime Minister Brian Mulroney was noticeably absent from the public eye. Some say he was drying out at a rehab clinic following a drinking binge. It remains as gossip and hearsay. What is not hearsay is the fact that the action at Oka followed the Latin American model for oppressive government action; a military representing the wealthy attacks a vastly overpowered indigenous population in order to seize land and/ or resources from them.

18 Throughout the "Manufacturing Consent" section, it was convenient to use different examples as the show developed, and as its focus shifted. Because the variations are too numerous to include in their entirety (there is an infinitude of

examples of media distortions), we will present but one alternate reading for "Choice of Topic":

BROOKS Throughout the years of Sandinista rule, one consistent choice of topic was the shipment of arms from the Sandinistas to Salvadorean guerrillas. The US government advanced this bit of misinformation in order to activate the domestic population's fear of Communism. There is nothing more convenient than the threat of the spread of International Communism for the American government to justify its foreign policy. In fact, there exists no evidence that the Sandinista government was indeed shipping arms to the guerrillas. However, evidence does exist to suggest that the contras were shipping guns to the guerrillas for a tidy profit. Who bought the guns initially? The American taxpayer.

Demonstration of Choice of Topic.

Guillermo?

VERDECCHIA Yes?

BROOKS Do you do drugs?

VERDECCHIA Well...yes.

BROOKS Did you do drugs or have a drink at any time during the creation of this play?

VERDECCHIA Well, I may have had an Armagnac...

BROOKS How many women have you slept with?

VERDECCHIA I don't keep count.

BROOKS Guillermo, did you not tell me on the night of December 3, 1989, and I quote, "It really pisses me off that *Love and Anger* is touted as a controversial and dangerous play. It's not. I mean, it's got some witty things in it but really, it's not—"

VERDECCHIA Daniel—

BROOKS And then did you not say on January 10, 1990, when I asked you how it was going with *Amigo's Blue Guitar*, a play you were working on at the Tarragon Theatre, did you not answer, and I quote, "I can't afford to be critical of a play when I am working on it." And when I told you I would be quoting you on this stage, did you not say, and I quote, "I'll never work again," more concerned with your career than with anything else. No, Mr. Ver*decchia*, the issue here has nothing to do with your paranoid ideas about thought control in a democratic society, and *everything* to do with your tendency towards alcoholism, womanizing, drug addiction, and gross hypocrisy...

19 Paul Robinson's review of Chomsky's *Language and Responsibility*, begins: "Judged in terms of the power, range, novelty, and influence of his thought, Noam Chomsky is arguably the most important intellectual alive today. He is also a disturbingly divided intellectual. On the one hand there is a large body of revolutionary and highly technical linguistic scholarship, much of it too difficult for anyone but the professional linguist or philosopher; on the other, an equally substantial body of political writings, accessible to any literate person but often maddeningly simple-minded."

20 For an in-depth analysis of the Israeli-Palestinian conflict, see Chomsky's *The Fateful Triangle* (Black Rose Books, 1984).

21 This was White House Spokesman Marlin Fitzwater's response to the destruction of a bomb shelter that killed as many as five hundred Iraqi civilians.

22 For Verdecchia's performance in the play *Jesus, Confucius and John Lennon*.

23 For Brooks' performance in John Mighton's play *Possible Worlds*.

24 The "Auction" section serves as a response to the "Any questions?" section (see note 9). The following was written for the DuMaurier World Stage performance:

BROOKS First let me state that freedom of the press exists for those who own one, and we own this show. Second, I'd like to go back to the contract question if I may Guillermo, by way of a few statistics:

Ratio of cocaine seized by the Columbian military to that seized by Columbian police: one to four.

Ratio of emergency US aid received by the Columbian military to that received by the Columbian police: six to one.

Estimated number of Americans killed by illegal drugs a year: ten thousand.

Estimated number of Americans killed by Marlboro cigarettes a year: seventy-five thousand.

In 1986, an estimated one billion people world-wide smoked one trillion cigarettes resulting in 2.5 million deaths attributable to smoking. *But* per capita smoking is declining in the USA and Canada, so tobacco companies are pressing advertising in Third World countries (including the Third World of Inner City, USA), where per capita smoking has increased by 76 percent. In Third World countries, where education and literacy are much neglected, and money, instead of going to education, goes to Swiss bank accounts, tobacco companies still insist that there is no conclusive proof of a causal relationship between smoking and ill health, even though we have as evidence everything but a signed confession from a cigarette. Now, Guillermo, is the derogation of the entire tobacco industry considered a breach of contract, and if so, does it matter, as we have already received our paycheques?

The following was written after the firing of Guy Sprung (see the second part of note 9).

BROOKS   I would like to come back to this Canadian Stage thing if I may, Guillermo.

Jim Leech, the president of Canadian Stage, has taken a lot of flack for the springing of Sprung, and in the spirit of fair play, I would like to come to his defence.

First, Leech says that Canadian Stage's two million dollar deficit is, and I quote, "not a lot of money." Who can argue with him? The thirty-seven million dollar profit of Unicorp Canada Corporation, of which Mr. Leech is president, now that's a lot of money.

Second, though Mr. Leech and the board of Canadian Stage may have made some mistakes, I would like to defend Mr. Leech by saying that he is a very busy man.

He is chairman of Mark Resources Incorporated, director and president of Union Enterprises Limited, vice-chairman of Union Gas Limited, senior vice-president and director of Unicorp American Corporation, and a director of the Lincoln Savings Bank. All these companies are subsidiaries of Unicorp Canada Corporation, of which he is president.

The company is now very busy reorganizing because it is being taken over by Brascan, which owns a chunk of Noranda mines (among other things).

Last year, Unicorp was busy trying to buy out Dunkin' Donuts in partnership with Cara Operations, owners of the busy Swiss Chalet and Harvey's (among other things).

Leech is also director of the Harris Steel Group Inc., and of Midland Doherty Financial, which recently had a busy merger with Walwyn Inc.

He is a trustee of Queen's University, and a member of the Ranchmen's Club, the Glencoe Club, the National Club and the Granite Club, which, by the way, now does take Jewish members, which, I am pleased to say, makes me a prospective member.

Jim Leech is a busy man, and if his interests are not exactly aligned with the special interests of socialists, union people, the unemployed, visible minorities, bearded people, if his interests are not exactly the same as yours or mine, you can hardly blame him, he is a very busy man.

25 As of June 1991, *The Noam Chomsky Lectures* had been performed thirty-five times to an audience of approximately twenty-six hundred people. This particular audience opinion poll has always been a part of the show. Of those twenty-six hundred people, only two have responded by raising a hand. One was a founder of Theatre Passe Muraille.

26 Written especially for publication in *what* magazine, March 1990.

VERDECCHIA Daniel will fall down a number of times while I speak, and each time he falls down will represent 100 political assassinations carried out in the country of Guatemala over a one-year period, assassinations carried out with American support as well as Canadian loans and Canadian arms. Anytime, Daniel.

[BROOKS *begins to fall as* VERDECCHIA *speaks and counts the falls with his hands*]

You will notice an absence of informed reporting on Guatemala in our press. Amnesty International tells us that since 1988 abuses have escalated resulting in hundreds of victims of so-called disappearances. You will find no reports on the murder and torture of hundreds of Peruvians at the hands of Peruvian security forces. Our media prefers instead to focus on the "Maoist-Terrorist" Sendero Luminoso. And try as you might, you will find next to nothing on East Timor, where an entire country has been annexed and where a quarter-of-a-million people have been annihilated by Indonesia, a country that buys a lot of arms from Canada.

This silence compared to revelations of corruption in Eastern Bloc countries, or the attention given to Salman Rushdie, or the opening of *The Phantom of the Opera* (a front-page article in *The Globe*) reveals clearly the boundaries within which our media operates. And let us not forget the advertising revenue that will be received by *The Globe* from *The Phantom* in the coming months, or years, or, God forbid, decades.

[VERDECCHIA *has counted twelve falls.* BROOKS *rises, brushes himself off, checks contributions to the Poindexter Defense Fund, and throws some change into the hat*]

Written for the DuMaurier World Stage performance:

VERDECCHIA Daniel has just fallen down. He will fall down a number of times while I speak. Each time he falls will represent 100 Panamanians killed during the American invasion. The figure we arrive at is a conservative estimate.

Let's talk about photographs. Looking back, we see that absolutely no photographs showing the effects of US bombardment in Panama City were run in our newspapers during the invasion last year. Yet somehow, we manage to get photographs of Chinese protestors being dragged off by soldiers.

Let's talk about Salman Rushdie and Farzad Bazoft. In the past year, numerous articles have been devoted to the death threat against Salman Rushdie. And in one day, we had four articles on the execution of British journalist Farzad Bazoft, accused of spying by the Iraqi government. Yet, how many articles do we read on the dozens of journalists executed in Guatemala and El Salvador? Why have we heard nothing about the five thousand Panamanians being held in detention camps by the US army?

This silence, compared to the attention given to Madonna's chipped tooth, reveals the ideological boundaries that our mainstream press operates within.

27 Written shortly after the Nicaraguan elections:

VERDECCHIA Ladies and gentlemen, it has been my experience that a review in *The Toronto Star* can make or break a show at the box office. I find that worrisome, because the writing in this paper descends to incredibly stupid depths at times. In an article about the president-elect of Nicaragua, we are told that Violetta Chamorro leads a life of pain, "yet she is cheerful and has been known to sing arias from operas to her friends." In Henry Mietkiewicz' review of the play *Potestad*, he misses the point and tells us that Argentina's Dirty War is a familiar subject and that the playwright ran the risk of turning his play into a "tedious, political rant." I would like to suggest that most of us, including Mr. Mietkiewicz, don't know *shit* about the dirty war, and I would like to know what the fuck is wrong with a political rant anyway you— [*he smashes the Artstick on the desk*]

28 When Robert Crew was *The Toronto Star* drama critic, we had quoted him as saying, "I didn't ever get to grips with the central themes being presented." (see note 7). Hence, we ended the marketing section by saying:

BROOKS And finally on the poster, a quote from *Toronto Star* theatre critic Robert Crew that will read:
dot dot dot GRIPS dot dot dot.

29 Based on a series of stories in Eduardo Galeano's *Memory of Fire, Vol. III: Century of the Wind* (Pantheon Books, 1988).

30 From the introduction to Chomsky's *Turning the Tide* (Black Rose Books, 1987).

Select Bibliography

By Noam Chomsky

American Power and the New Mandarins. New York: Pantheon Books, 1969.

The Culture of Terrorism. Boston: South End Press, 1988.

The Fateful Triangle: The United Staes, Israel and the Palestinians. Montreal: Black Rose Books, 1984.

Language and Politics. Ed. Carlos P. Otero. Montreal: Black Rose Books, 1988.

Language and Responsibility. New York: Pantheon Books, 1979.

Necessary Illusions: Thought Control in Democratic Societies. Montreal: CBC Enterprises, 1989.

On Power and Ideology: The Managua Lectures. Boston: South End Press, 1987.

Pirates and Emperors: Internatioanl Terrorism in the Real World. Montreal: Black Rose Books, 1987.

Reflections on Language. New York: Pantheon Books, 1975.

Towards a New Cold War: Essays on the Current Crisis and How We Got There. New York: Pantheon Books, 1982.

Turning the Tide: US Intervention in Central America and the Struggle for Peace. Montreal: Black Rose Books, 1987.

By Noam Chomsky and Edward S. Herman

Manufacturing Consent: The Political Economy of the Mass Media. New York: Pantheon Books, 1988.

The Political Economy of Human Rights, Vol. I: The Washington Connection and Third World Fascism. Boston: South End Press, 1979.

The Political Economy of Human Rights, Vol. II: After the Cataclysm: Postwar Indochina and the Reconstruction of Imperial Ideology. Boston: South End Press, 1979.

On Media

Bagdikian, Ben. *The Media Monopoly.* Boston: Beacon Press, 1987.

Desbarats, Peter. *Guide to the Canadian News Media.* Toronto: Harcourt Brace Jovanovich, 1990.

Lee, Martin and Norman Solomon. *Unreliable Sources: A Guide to Checking Bias in News Media.* New York: Carol Pub. Group, 1991.

Siegel, Arthur. *Politics and the Media in Canada.* Toronto: McGraw-Hill Ryerson, 1982.

On Canada

Brecher, Irving, ed. *Human Rights, Development, and Foreign Policy: Canadian Perspectives.* Halifax, NS: Institute for Research on Public Policy, 1989.

Clement, Wallace. *The Canadian Corporate Elite.* Ottawa: Carleton University Press, 1986.

The Financial Post's Directory of Directors. Toronto: The Financial Post, 1991.

Levant, Victor. *Quiet Complicity.* Toronto: Between the Lines, 1986.

Matthews, Robert O. and Cranford Pratt, eds. *Human Rights in Canadian Foreign Policy.* Montreal: McGill-Queen's University Press, 1988.

McFarlane, Peter. *Northern Shadows: Canadians and Central America.* Toronto: Between the Lines, 1989.

Nelson, Joyce. *Sultans of Sleaze: P.R., Pollsters and the Media.* Toronto: Between the Lines, 1989.

Newman, Peter C. *The Bronfman Dynasty: The Rothschilds of the New World.* Toronto: McClelland and Stewart, 1978.

———. *The Canadian Establishment, Vol. I.* Toronto: McClelland and Stewart, 1978.

———. *The Canadian Establishment, Vol. II: The Acquisitors.* Toronto: McClelland and Stewart, 1989.

Sawatsky, John. *The Insiders: Power, Money and Secrets in Ottawa.* Toronto: McLelland and Stewart, 1989.

Who's Who In Canada. Toronto: International Press Ltd., 1991.

Who's Who In Canadian Business. Toronto: Trans-Canada, 1990.

On the Middle East

Binur, Yoram. *My Enemy, Myself.* New York: Doubleday, 1989.

Lockman, Zachary and Joel Beinin, eds. *Intifada: The Palestinian Uprising Against Israeli Occupation.* Boston: South End Press, 1989.

Odeh, B.J. *Lebanon: Dynamics of Conflict: A Modern Political History.*
London: Zed, 1989.

Rodinson, Maxine. *Israel: A Colonial-Settler State?* New York: Monad Press,
1973.

Schiff, Ze'ev and Ehud Ya'ari. *Intifada: The Palestinian Uprising—Israel's
Third Front.* New York: Touchstone, 1990.

Schmidt, Dana A. *Armageddon in the Middle East.* New York: John Day
Co., 1974.

On Latin America

Barry, Tom and Deb Preusch. *The Central America Fact Book.* New York:
Grove Press, 1986.

Galeano, Eduardo. *Memory of Fire, Vol. I: Genesis.* New York: Pantheon
Books, 1987.

————. *Memory of Fire, Vol. II: Faces and Masks.* New York: Pantheon
Books, 1988.

————. *Memory of Fire, Vol. III: Century of the Wind.* New York:
Pantheon Books, 1988.

————. *The Open Veins of Latin America: Five Centuries of the Pillage of a
Continent.* New York: Monthly Review Press, 1973.

Leiken, Robert and Barry Rubin, eds. *The Central American Crisis Reader.*
New York: Summit Books, 1987.

Other Books

Cockburn, Alexander. *Corruptions of Empire: Life Studies and the Reagan
Empire.* New York: Verso, 1987.

Herman, Edward S. and Gerry O'Sullivan. *The Terrorism Industry: The
Experts and Institutes that Shape Our View of Terror.* New York:
Pantheon Books, 1990.

Korner, Peter et al. *The IMF and the Debt Crisis: A Guide to the Third
World's Dilemma.* Trans. Paul Knight. London: Zed, 1986.

Publications

The Activist.
Americas Watch Reports.
Amnesty International: Annual Reports.
Annual Reports of Various Corporations.
Barricada.
Canadian Dimension.

The Economist.
Fuse.
Harper's.
In These Times.
Inter-Church Committee on Human Rights in Latin America: Annual Reports.
International Journal.
Jornada.
Journal of Palestine Studies.
Lies of Our Times.
The MacKenzie Institute Newsletter.
Maclean's.
The Manchester Guardian.
Newsweek.
Opinion Cultural.
Policy Options.
Ploughshares.
Resource Center Bulletins.
Taskforce on the Churches and Corporate Responsibility: Annual Reports.
This Magazine.
Time.
Z Magazine.

Daily Newspapers
The Globe and Mail.
The Los Angeles Times.
The New York Post.
The New York Times.
The Toronto Star.
The Toronto Sun.

Consultations With
Harold Hickman, Department of External Affairs
The Prime Minister's Office
Ken Epps, Project Ploughshares
SalvAide
Canadian Action for Nicaragua
Gossip With Friends

... some of the fundamentals of theatre, like communication, honest emotion, engagement and commitment to the characters on the stage.
-Robert Crew,
Toronto Star, June 14/90

The Authors

Daniel Brooks studied theatre in Toronto, the "Method" in New York, clown in Paris, dance in Buenos Aires and puppet theatre in Brazil. He has performed his own work in Europe and South America, and worked with many theatre companies in Toronto as a writer, director, and actor. He is currently Artistic Co-Director of Toronto's Augusta Company.

Guillermo Verdecchia is an Argentinian-born actor and writer whose work has been seen on stages across Canada. He is the author of *Final Decisions (War)* and co-author, with members of the Canadian Stage Hour Co., of *i.d.*, an award-winning play for young audiences dealing with racism and police violence.

Editor for the Press: Jason Sherman
Cover Design: Reactor
Production Still: John Anderson

Coach House Press
401 (rear) Huron Street
Toronto, Canada
M5S 2G5